RAF

A HISTORY OF THE ROYAL AIR FORCE
THROUGH ITS AIRCRAFT

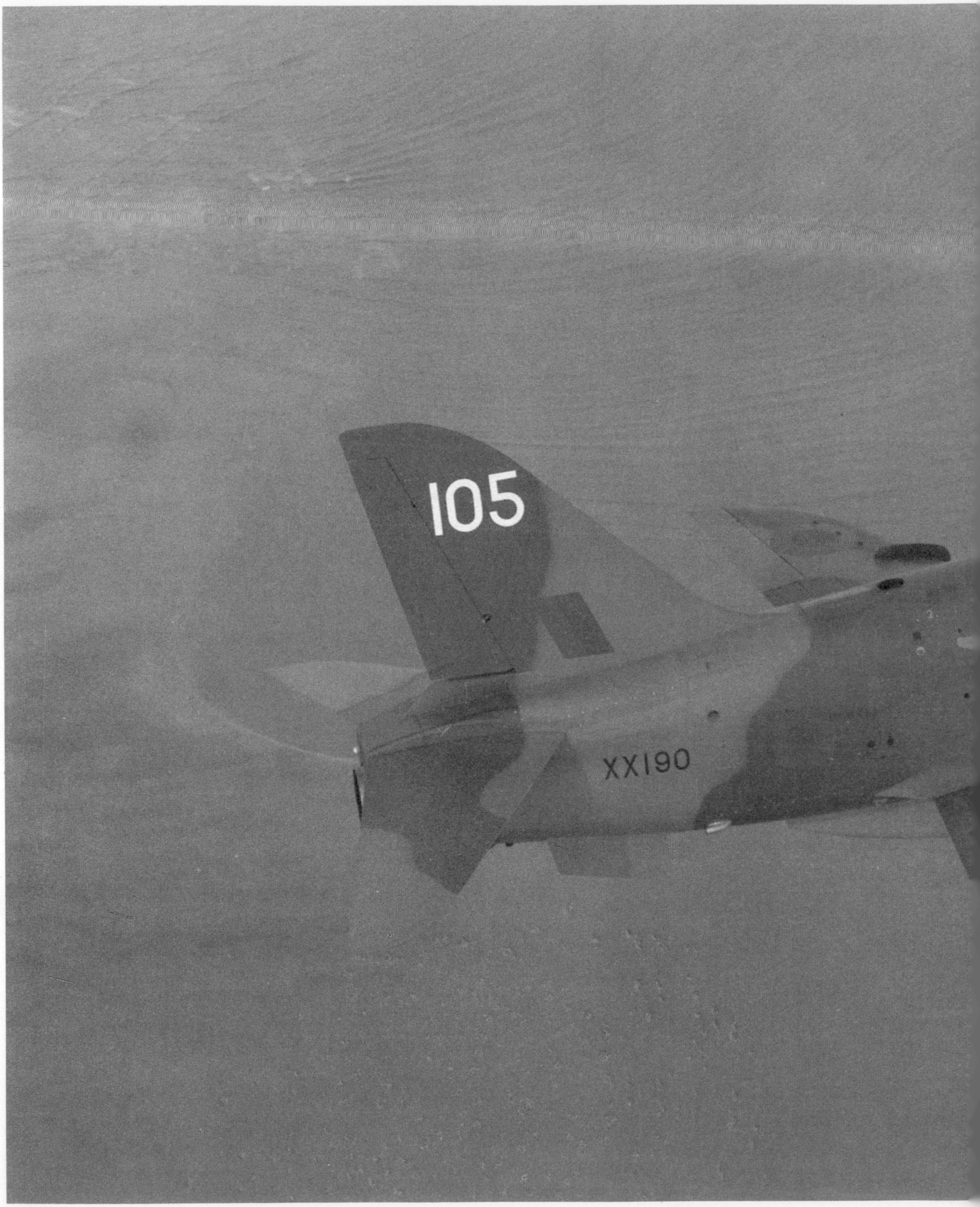
105
XX190

RAF

A HISTORY OF THE ROYAL AIR FORCE THROUGH ITS AIRCRAFT

BERNARD FITZSIMONS

WINDWARD

© 1983 Winchmore Publishing Services Limited

First published by Windward
An imprint owned by
W. H. Smith & Sons Limited
Registered No. 237811 England

Trading as W.H.S. Distributors,
St. John's House,
East Street,
Leicester LE1 6NE

Produced by Winchmore Publishing Services Limited,
40 Triton Square,
London NW1.

ISBN 0 7112 0324 5

Designed by Pierre Tilley

Printed in Hong Kong

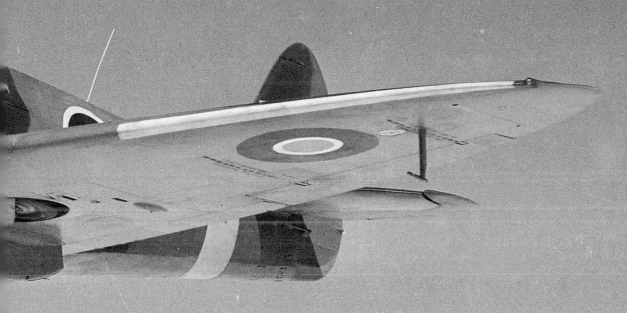

1 FORMATION

By 1 April 1918 the First World War was drawing towards the end of its fourth year. Across Belgium and northern France, from the shores of the English Channel to the borders of Switzerland, were networks of defensive positions built up over three and a half years of trench warfare: during March the opening attacks of the last great German offensive had pushed back the Allied lines to the south of Arras, and the air battles that had accompanied the fighting on the ground were only just dying away.

Nevertheless, the flying and the fighting continued, and as dawn broke over the Western Front the first patrols were taking off. Reconnaissance aircraft began their work of seeking out targets for the artillery and photographing the German positions. Fighters crossed the lines on offensive patrols, engaging German aircraft as they found them or attacking targets on the ground. Bombers battled their way through anti-aircraft fire to strike at bridges and airfields. Throughout the day the activity continued, and even after dusk the night bombers began to take off on their missions, heading towards their objectives under cover of darkness.

The statistics for the day were not untypical. The total of 49 reconnaissance missions had included three long-distance flights, and eight squadrons mounting bombing raids during the day had dropped 451 bombs between them, with a total weight of nearly 16,000 lb (7257 kg). The fighter patrols had claimed a total of 13 enemy aircraft destroyed, with another 10 listed as out of control. In turn, 11 British aircraft had been shot down by their German opponents, while another six were lost to ground fire, and after dark

Previous page: 'Closing Up', by George Davis, showing D.H.4 day bombers under attack

Above: A preserved example of one of the finest fighters of the First World War, the S.E.5a

three of No 101 Squadron's F.E.2b night bombers were damaged in an air raid on their base at Haute Visée. Total casualties included three dead, two of them killed in the same air raid, and another 14 aircrew missing.

Enemy action was not the only cause of aircraft losses. Five machines crashed on take-off and another 14 crashed on landing. Four were forced down with engine trouble and another had to make an emergency landing in a storm, while enemy ground fire damaged a further five. A total of 28 damaged aircraft were returned to depots for repair, while 21 were wrecked, abandoned or failed to return from their offensive patrols.

On that first day of April, however, there was one significant difference. The orders for the day had not come from the War Office or the Admiralty, but from a new organisation named the Air Ministry. The Royal Flying Corps and Royal Naval Air Service, hitherto branches of the army and navy respectively, were now united in a third service, called the Royal Air Force and charged with the defence of the realm by air and the conduct of all air operations.

The four squadrons of the Royal Flying Corps that had gone to France with the British Expeditionary Force in August 1914 comprised 860 officers and men with 63 aeroplanes. Another 116 aeroplanes were left behind in England, where the Royal Naval Air Service, originally the Naval Wing of the RFC, with its coastal bases in southern England, was responsible for the air defence of Great Britain. In that year barely 200 new aircraft were produced in Britain.

The tiny air force in France made an immediate

9

S.E.5as under construction at the
Wolseley factory in Birmingham.
More than 5000 S.E.5as were
produced by several manufacturers
during the last two years of the
war, and it served with 25 RAF
squadrons during 1918

contribution to the survival of the BEF, its reconnaissance sorties giving warning of German attacks as the early retreat from Mons was followed by the battles of the Marne and Ypres and the digging of trenches. Thereafter aircraft were used in support of the ground forces by spotting for the artillery and providing aerial reconnaissance reports. As their power increased they were adapted to carry radios for communicating with the gun batteries, cameras to photograph enemy positions, small bombs to harass the opposing ground forces and light machine guns for self-defence.

The tactics of aerial fighting were refined gradually, and bombing attacks began to be co-ordinated with the activities of the ground forces, and as the demand for new aircraft continued to grow production was increased dramatically. The Royal Aircraft Factory at Farnborough, where Lieutenant-Colonel Hugh Trenchard was in charge of building up supplies of aircraft and pilots, continued its experimental work, and private constructors joined in. During 1915 more than 2000 aircraft were built, the number rising to over 6000 in 1916 and over 14,000 by 1917.

However British aviation before the outbreak of war had been outstripped by French, German and Italian efforts, and it was not long before German aircraft began to carry out raids across the Channel. A bomb was dropped from a seaplane near Dover in December 1914, and the following month Zeppelin airships carried out attacks on towns along the east coast. By May 1915 the Zeppelins were attacking London itself, and further attacks followed, though the destruction caused was somewhat random.

Early in 1916 the responsibility for home defence returned to the RFC and effective anti-aircraft fire, allied to such refinements as incendiary and explosive bullets for aircraft machine guns, forced the airships to fly higher and higher, diminishing the effectiveness of their raids. By October 1916 mounting losses had persuaded the German High Command to disband the army airship force, and while naval airships continued to mount sporadic raids, the emphasis changed to aeroplane attacks. The range limitations that had

confined early aeroplane raids to eastern Kent were being overcome with the development of twin-engined aircraft designated G for Grosskampfflugzeuge, or big combat aircraft.

The first raids by the new bombers, on 25 May and 5 June 1917, turned back because of the weather, dropping their bombs on Folkestone and Sheerness, but on 13 June a formation of 20 Gotha G.Vs, flying at a height of 15,000 ft (4572 m), dropped a total of 72 bombs on the City of London and the East End, killing 162 people and injuring more than 400, arousing public alarm and exacerbating the political controversy over home defence that had largely died down with the successes achieved against the airships. A second raid on 7 July repeated the pattern of the first, and while casualties were lower, the Germans' apparent ability to attack London at will was enough to trigger off riots in the East End.

The renewed debate highlighted problems of both equipment and organisation. The B.E.2cs used by the home defence squadrons provided a stable platform for attacks on airships, but were simply incapable of climbing to the Gothas' altitude quickly enough to intercept them, and their single machine guns were no match for the bombers' massed fire from three machine guns each. Moreover, the tactics that had been evolved for countering the Zeppelins, using searchlights on the ground to illuminate them for artillery and aircraft, were inadequate to deal with the smaller, faster bombers. Interceptions were attempted by scores of aircraft, but as individuals without precise details of the enemy's whereabouts they had little chance of finding them. Immediate reactions included the return of No 56 Squadron, with its S.E.5s, to England, and the relocation of No 66 Squadron, with Sopwith Camels, to Dunkirk, and there were calls for increases in aircraft production and Cabinet approval for an increase in the size of the RFC from 128 to 200 squadrons.

However, it was clear that a full reappraisal of the role of the RFC and RNAS was called for: aircraft were equally in demand on the Western Front, and the two borrowed squadrons had already returned there before the second raid on London. Accordingly, the prime minister, David Lloyd George, set up a committee under the South African General Jan Smuts to investigate 'Air Organisation and Home Defence against Air Raids'.

As far as home defence was concerned, the committee recommended that a single, unified command should be established to control all anti-aircraft operations. This was approved by the Cabinet, and on 5 August Brigadier-General E B Ashmore was appointed to command the London Air Defence Area, encompassing both anti-aircraft batteries and the aircraft elements, including three new squadrons intended to fight in formation rather than as individuals. Further German bomber raids were made by night in September and October, but as the defences were strengthened the Gothas and the new Zeppelin-Staaken Giants began to suffer losses caused both by ground fire and by aircraft, and during the first half of 1918 the raids gradually petered out.

Meanwhile, the final report of the Smuts committee was signed on 17 August 1917, and this contained some even more far-reaching recommendations. Central to these was the proposal that a separate service should be established to take over the RFC and RNAS, with a new department of state to be responsible for it. This was not the first such suggestion, and a number of earlier attempts had been made to co-ordinate the efforts of the military and naval air arms with those of the aircraft manufacturers. In February 1916 the Joint War Air Committee had been established under Lord Derby, and in May this was replaced by the Air Board under Lord Curzon, but neither organisation had any real power, and both saw the establishment of a separate service under a new air ministry as the only real solution to the conflicting demands of the existing air arms.

A second Air Board was established at the beginning of 1917, under the new government of Lloyd George, with Lord Cowdray as its president, and this time it was given responsibility for the design of aircraft and engines. To this end the new committee included both Commodore G M Paine, the new head of the RNAS, who became Fifth Sea Lord, and Lieutenant-General Sir David Henderson, Director-General of Military Aviation, as well as William Weir, of the Glasgow engineering firm G & J Weir, who became Controller of Aeronautical Supplies. In an attempt to end the inter-service rivalry over aircraft, a new unified headquarters was set up to house both military and naval procurement executives, along with representatives of the Ministry of Munitions, which continued to be responsible for the manufacture of aircraft.

The second board went some way to improving the position. Prototypes of the Royal Aircraft Factory's S.E.5 and the Sopwith Camel had been flown for the first time towards the end of 1916, and during 1917 production of single-seaters began to be concentrated on these two types, though shortages of engines continued to delay deliveries.

In spite of these improvements, the Air Board was

Detail from 'Panorama of the Western Front' by W G Wyllie. Manoeuvring for a shot with a hand aimed machine gun was made easier by putting the gunner in front and the propeller behind, but synchronised guns were the real answer

still greatly handicapped. Its responsibility was limited to the selection and design of new aircraft. The RFC and RNAS decided their own policies, and production remained in the hands of the Ministry of Munitions. Cowdray, too, believed that only the creation of a separate air service could provide an effective solution to the administrative difficulties involved, though he did not consider such a drastic reorganisation possible until the war was over. Smuts was more sanguine, and the Cabinet was now ready to agree, almost immediately, Henderson was appointed to head an Air Organisation Committee to be responsible for the detailed planning for the new service.

In October 1917 Henderson resigned his post as Director-General of Military Aviation, and was replaced by Major-General John Salmond, hitherto in command of the Training Division. Another month brought the publication of the Air Force (Constitution) Bill, which became law on 29 November. The date for establishing the new organisation was fixed for April 1918, and Lord Rothermere, the newspaper proprietor, became Secretary of State for Air. By the end of the year an Air Council had been appointed under Rothermere, with Henderson as vice-president. Salmond, meanwhile, assumed command of the RFC in the field, replacing Major-General Sir Hugh Trenchard, who returned to London to become Chief of the Air Staff.

The function of the Air Council was to act, under the presidency of the Air Minister (Secretary of State), as an advisory board to the Air Ministry, while the Air Staff assumed responsibility for operations, including planning, intelligence and training. As originally constituted, in January 1918, the Air Council included Rothermere, Henderson, Trenchard and his deputy, plus the individuals in charge of personnel, equipment, aircraft production and works and buildings. Post-war Air Councils generally had fewer members: from 1925 the normal membership included the Secretary of State and his deputy, the Chief of the Air Staff, and Air Members, as they were termed, for Personnel and for Supply and Research. From 1935 the last responsibility was divided, separate members having responsibility for Research and Development and for Supply and Organisation.

Unfortunately, the new ministry was more imposing in name than in substance. Established in improvised offices in the Hotel Cecil, it was handicapped by lack of staff and lack of official policy, and immediately found itself under pressure from army, navy, government and public opinion. Trenchard, who had been responsible for building up the RFC from the Royal Aircraft Factory at Farnborough, and who had become its field commander at the end of 1915, was essentially hostile to the idea of a separate force and intolerant of outside advice. The result was his resignation in March 1918, followed by that of Henderson when Major-General Frederick Sykes, a senior staff officer who had been the first field commander of the Military Wing of the RFC, replaced Trenchard.

Rothermere himself would last only a few more weeks, resigning on 25 April to be replaced by Weir, but in the meantime the transfer of the RFC and RNAS had to go ahead: the date was set for 1 April, and on 7 March it was announced in a royal proclamation that the new service would be named the Royal Air Force.

Naturally, the basic requirement for an air force, royal or otherwise, is aeroplanes. In August 1914 the RFC had been able to muster a total of 197, and there was no real aircraft industry in Britain. During 1915 nearly 2000 new aeroplanes were produced, with a further 470 being bought from French sources and another 264 ordered from Curtiss in the United States. Production was trebled during 1916, but it was only in 1917, with the appointment of the Second Air Board, that design and manufacture began to be organised on a coherent basis.

The procedure established was that the War Office and Admiralty should make their plans for the RFC and RNAS in consultation with the Air Board, whose Technical Department was responsible for issuing specifications to manufacturers, assessing and checking the designs submitted, and ordering prototypes. Orders for production aircraft were placed by the Ministry of Munitions, using blueprints supplied by the Technical Department. The Air Board's Controller of Aeronautical Supplies was also responsible for allocating or approving orders for materials and components, many of which were supplied by a growing number of sub-contractors. Production at the Royal Aircraft Factory, Farnborough, had been suspended in 1916, but experimental and design work continued there.

Of course, the new system was not immune from bureaucratic clumsiness, but it did result in a vital rationalisation of production, not least by imposing a degree of standardisation both on the variety of aircraft types and on those used by the two flying services. The result was that by April 1918 on the Western Front the vast majority of the 57 RFC and 16 RNAS squadrons united in the new air force were equipped with only a handful of designs.

The actual numbers of aircraft varied constantly – wastage of single-seat fighters, for example, averaged 66 per cent per month during 1918 – but one of the most common aircraft in use by front-line squadrons was the R.E.8, which equipped 14 former RFC squadrons. Designed at the Royal Aircraft Factory, and numbered in the Reconnaissance Experimental series, the R.E.8 became known as the Harry Tate after a music-hall comedian of the day. More than 2000 were used in France between its introduction towards the end of 1916 and the end of the war, and in the Corps Reconnaissance role their duties in support of the ground forces were extremely varied. Standard tasks were reconnaissance and spotting for the artillery – designating targets for the gunners and transmitting instructions to the batteries to correct their aim – while photographic reconnaissance became increasingly important, and message and supply dropping

A line-up of Royal Aircraft Factory products at Farnborough. On the left are four B.E.2cs interspersed with two B.E.12s and a B.E.2a, and the line continues with an F.E.8, an S.E.4a, two F.E.2bs, two R.E.8s and an R.E.7

The Shuttleworth Trust's Avro
504K, modified from an original
504N by Avro apprentices in 1951

were common. The R.E.8 was also used for ground attacks, being armed with a fixed forward-firing Vickers gun and one or two Lewis guns in the rear cockpit and able to carry 260 lb (118 kg) of bombs. Its inherent stability was useful for the slow, regular course required in artillery observation work, though its limited performance, with a top speed of 102 mph (164 km/h), made it somewhat vulnerable.

The other Corps Reconnaissance aircraft was the Armstrong Whitworth F.K.8, designed by Frederik Koolhoven and introduced into service in France in January 1917. The F.K.8 carried a similar gun armament to that of the R.E.8; known as the Big Ack, it was employed for the same tasks and was generally regarded as the better aeroplane and could carry up to 400 lb (181 kg) of bombs, although it equipped only four squadrons in France in April 1918 and only some 1500 were built, compared with over 4000 R.E.8s.

One Corps Reconnaissance squadron was still equipped with B.E.2cs, though these were replaced by R.E.8s in May. The Royal Aircraft Factory's second 'Bleriot Experimental', so designated by virtue of its having a tractor propeller, as used by the French aviator, rather than a pusher, was produced in large numbers and a number of variants, the first of which dated from as early as 1912. The later versions, last of which was the B.E.2e, first flown in mid-1916, were sadly outdated by the time they appeared, and performance with their 90-hp RAF 1a engines was so poor, with a maximum speed of only 72 mph (116 km/h), that large numbers were shot down by German fighters.

Another of the aircraft designed in 1916 as a replacement for the B.E.2, the Bristol R.2A, was transformed by the addition of a synchronised machine gun into the F.2A, and with the 275-hp Rolls-Royce Falcon III engine it became the F.2B, though many F.2Bs had other engines which gave inferior performance. After a shaky start in action on the Western Front in April 1917, the pilots realised that the new type was much faster and more manoeuvrable than existing reconnaissance aircraft, and with its synchronised machine gun could be flown as a single-seat fighter, the observer in the rear cockpit providing tail cover with his Lewis guns. In July 1917 it was decided that the F.2B should be the standard fighter-reconnaissance machine. By April 1918 five squadrons were using the Bristol Fighter, as it was named officially, or the Brisfit as it was known to its crews; another joined them during the month, and long-range artillery-spotting flights also used it. The fighter-reconnaissance role involved deeper penetration of enemy airspace than the standard reconnaissance over the lines, and the F.2B's fighting ability made it ideally suited to the job. The F.2Bs of No 22 Squadron carried out the first RAF sorties on the morning of 1 April.

Reconnaissance and artillery spotting had been the original roles of aircraft in the war – indeed, the only ones in which they could make a useful contribution in the early stages – and their success soon inspired

An F.E.2b of No 100 Squadron ready to take off on a night bombing raid. Originally a fighter-reconnaissance type, the F.E.2b was switched to night bombing when it became outclassed in its original role

A852

attempts to interfere with their work. With the addition of machine guns aeroplanes acquired the ability to destroy other aircraft, and this in turn led to the development of specialised fighting aircraft, essentially high-performance, armed single-seaters, used to attack and defend more vulnerable reconnaissance types and, later, bombers.

During 1918 the standard British fighters were the Sopwith Camel and the S.E.5a, another Royal Aircraft Factory design. The first prototype F.1 Camel was flown in December 1916, and with the torque of its 110-hp Clerget rotary engine (production aircraft used a variety of nine-cylinder rotaries) accentuated by the concentration of pilot, engine and twin Vickers guns in the forward fuselage it proved exceptionally manoeuvrable, though by no means easy to handle.

having 200-hp Hispano-Suiza engines or British-built derivatives, by the time of the RAF's inception. Although less manoeuvrable than the Camel, the S.E.5a was correspondingly easier to fly, and its greater stability when diving made its armament of a single synchronised Vickers and a Lewis gun mounted above the upper wing effective at longer ranges.

Meanwhile, a new Sopwith fighter produced during 1917 had entered service at the beginning of 1918. The 5F.1 Dolphin was designed to carry a pair of Lewis guns firing upwards at 45° as well as a pair of synchronised Vickers guns, though the former were often discarded, and problems with the powerplant, the 200-hp geared Hispano-Suiza, meant that some 900 of the 1500 built had not entered service by the end of the war. Three squadrons were using the type on the

Naval squadrons were the first to receive the type, and by April 1918 eight former RFC and seven former RNAS squadrons were using the Camel on the Western Front. A total of nearly 3000 victories were claimed by Camels in the last 18 months of the war, a greater number than that for any other type, and two pilots each achieved the remarkable feat of shooting down six enemy aircraft in one day while flying Camels.

The fifth of the Farnborough Scouting Experimental aircraft was also flown in prototype form, with a 150-hp Hispano-Suiza V-8 engine, in December 1916 and had entered service in France with No 56 Squadron in April 1917. A further nine RFC squadrons on the Western Front had received S.E.5as, which differed from early production machines in

Western Front at the RAF's formation, and another arrived from England during that first month, and the type gave good service, primarily in escort and ground-attack work, often carrying four 20-lb (9-kg) bombs.

The only other Western Front fighter squadron using an alternative type, No 29, had its French-designed Nieuports replaced by S.E.5as in April 1918, but one earlier fighter-reconnaissance type remained in service in a new role. The Royal Aircraft Factory's F.E.2b, third in a series designated Farman Experimental because, with its pusher propeller, the first model had followed contemporary Farman design practice, had begun its career in France in September 1915, and the unobstructed forward field of fire enjoyed by the pillar-mounted Lewis guns provided for the pilot and observer enabled the F.E.2b, along with the Vickers F.B.5 'Gunbus' and Airco D.H.2, to put up a good resistance to the Fokker monoplanes of the day. The Fokkers were the first aircraft to be equipped with interrupter gear to allow their machine guns to fire forward through the propeller arc, giving them an immediate advantage over the conventional scouting aircraft which were forced to manoeuvre into position for the observers to use their manually aimed weapons.

As early as November 1916, by which time the F.E.2b was becoming outclassed as a fighter, the type began to be used for night bombing raids against air-fields and other targets behind the German lines. Their success in this role led to the formation of No 100 Squadron as a night-bombing unit in the spring of 1917, and by April 1918 a further four ex-RFC squadrons were using F.E.2bs for night-bombing raids over the Western Front, and another two followed during the next three months. For this task the F.E.2b was fitted with a simplified undercarriage, and it was able to carry loads ranging from 14 20-lb (9-kg) to a single 230-lb (104-kg) bomb.

In the meantime, purpose-built bombers had been developed, largely at the instigation of the RNAS,

which formed the 3rd Wing in the summer of 1916 for the specific purpose of bombing German munitions factories. Early in 1917 the wing received its first Handley Page O/100 bombers, which were also used by the long-range bombing squadrons of the 5th Wing.

When flown for the first time in December 1915 the O/100 was the biggest aeroplane yet built in Britain. A pair of 250-hp Rolls-Royce Eagle II engines powered the 100-ft (30.48-m) span biplane, whose wings had to be folded for accommodation in field hangars, and which carried a crew of five and up to 2000 lb (907 kg) of bombs. By April 1918 the four former RNAS squadrons equipped with the type had already begun converting to a more powerful derivative designated O/400. This was designed to use 360-hp Eagle IIIs, though other engines were substituted, and was used for night bombing until the end of the war.

While the giant bombers, along with the old F.E.2bs, were reserved for night operations, when darkness would help protect them from the attentions of German fighters, daylight bombing raids called for higher performance if unacceptably high losses were to be avoided. In this respect, one of the outstanding day bombers of the war, and one of the best of all combat aircraft, was the D.H.4, fourth of Geoffrey de Havilland's designs for the Aircraft Manufacturing Company.

Powered by a single 250-hp Rolls-Royce Eagle, the D.H.4 was capable of 130 mph (209 km/h) at 10,000 ft (3048 m), beyond the reach of all but the fastest German fighters, and later examples with 375-hp Eagles were capable of 143 mph (230 km/h) at sea level and a ceiling of 22,000 ft (6706 m). At the same time, its wooden construction gave it great strength, it was outstandingly responsive to the controls considering its span of 42 ft $4\frac{3}{4}$ in (12.9 m) and loaded weight of 3472 lb (1575 kg), including up to 460 lb (209 kg) of bombs. It also carried a useful armament of a forward-firing Vickers gun synchronised to fire through the propeller arc, and a Lewis gun in the observer's cockpit, which was well to the rear to give him an excellent field of fire. In fact, its only major drawback resulted from this last feature: with the pilot's cockpit well forward to give him the best possible view for bomb-aiming, communication between pilot and observer was impossible except by hand signals. In April 1918 six RFC and four RNAS squadrons in France brought D.H.4s into the Royal Air Force.

One of the main obstacles faced by aircraft designers at this time was the lack of either suitable engines or, when these existed, of adequate supplies. Figures for aircraft production during the war show that while some 55,000 airframes were constructed in Britain, only 41,000 engines were produced to power them. The numbers were made up largely by the purchase of nearly 17,000 foreign-built engines, principally from France; but often what engines were available proved deficient in power or unreliable in service.

These problems were illustrated by the disappointing D.H.9, designed as a successor to the D.H.4 with a 300-hp Siddeley Puma engine, longer range and a heavier bombload. Unfortunately, the new engine was based on the 230-hp Beardmore-Halford-Pul-

linger engine originally intended for the D.H.4 but replaced by the Eagle because of trouble with the BHP. In the event, the Puma itself only developed 230 hp, and the result was a dramatic reduction in performance, the only real improvement offered by the D.H.9 being easier communications between the crew members as a result of the cockpits being moved closer together – and even this involved restricting the pilot's view for bombing by the movement aft of his position. Nevertheless, large quantities of D.H.9s had been ordered in the expectation of improved performance, and by April 1918 the first two squadrons on the Western Front were flying the type.

By this stage of the war aircraft armament had been standardised, the two principal guns used being the Vickers and the Lewis, both of .303-in calibre. The Lewis was an air-cooled, drum-fed weapon of American origin which became the universal flexible gun on two-seat and bigger aircraft, where it was carried on a ring mounting designed by Warrant Officer F W Scarff. This mounting could be used for one or two guns and allowed them to be trained throughout the available field of fire.

Another mounting used for Lewis guns on single-seaters was the Foster, which carried the gun above the upper wing of a biplane; a rail allowed it to be pulled down towards the cockpit for changing the 47- or 97-round ammunition drums. This was no easy feat for a pilot who had to continue flying the aeroplane at the same time, but the Foster mount continued to be used on the S.E.5a and other aircraft until the end of the war. Another application of the Foster mount was

on night-fighter Camels, which mounted twin Lewis guns above the upper wing to avoid the flashes from the normal synchronised Vickers guns blinding the pilot, and to avoid the danger of incendiary and explosive ammunition in a synchronised gun.

The original purpose of the Foster mount was to allow the machine gun to be fixed in a forward-firing position clear of the propeller arc. Other solutions to the problem of installing a forward-firing gun without the danger of damage to the propeller included fitting the propeller blades with deflectors and mounting the gun between the cylinder banks of V-type engines to fire through the propeller shaft, but by 1918 interrupter gears to synchronise the gun's firing mechanism with the rotation of the propeller had dispensed with the need for such arrangements. The synchronising mechanism used on British aircraft was the Constantinesco CC gear, which involved a hydraulic linkage between the engine and the gun trigger, and one or two Vickers guns were standard on single-seat fighters and such two seaters as the Bristol Fighter and D.H.4. The Vickers was a belt-fed, air-cooled derivative of the original Maxim machine gun with a rate of fire of around 500 rds/min, though when synchronised its actual rate was governed by the rate of rotation of the propeller.

Several bigger guns were designed, and some even had special aircraft designed to use them, but the only heavy weapon to see service during the war was the Coventry Ordnance Works 1½-pounder, a 37-mm (1.46-in) weapon normally fed by five-round magazines. Other aircraft were built to carry recoilless

An early S.E.5a built by the Royal Aircraft Factory, showing the Lewis gun pulled down towards the cockpit on its Foster mount. Changing the ammunition drum was a difficult and hazardous operation

One of the Bristol Fighters
produced during the 1920s for army
co-operation work. In its original
role, the F.2B proved an
outstanding fighter-reconnaissance
aircraft, and remained in RAF
service until the early 1930s

guns, but the operational problems posed by the use of heavy weapons were never overcome satisfactorily.

Bombs and their associated aiming and release mechanisms had also made considerable progress since the first experiments with dropping grenades and other improvised projectiles over the sides of open cockpits. The requirements for a successful aircraft bomb include an aerodynamic shape that will produce a stable and predictable flight path, and a fuse and arming mechanism that will enable it to be carried safely yet detonate reliably. The RNAS had 20-lb (9-kg) Hale bombs, whose actual weight of $18\frac{1}{2}$ lb (8.39 kg) included only $4\frac{1}{2}$ lb of explosive, as early as 1913, and by 1915 100-lb (45-kg) were in service.

The Hale bomb's pear shape and stabilising tail fins represented the first efforts at giving a predictable trajectory, and the arming problem was solved by incorporating a small propeller in the tail. A safety clip to prevent this from turning while still attached to the aircraft was removed before launch, at first by hand but later by an automatic mechanism, and after release this was driven by its passage through the air to release the striker, allowing it to activate the detonator on impact.

The use of propellers to arm bombs in flight became standard practice, and as the weapons grew more sophisticated the flight distance needed to complete the arming sequence was made predictable. The

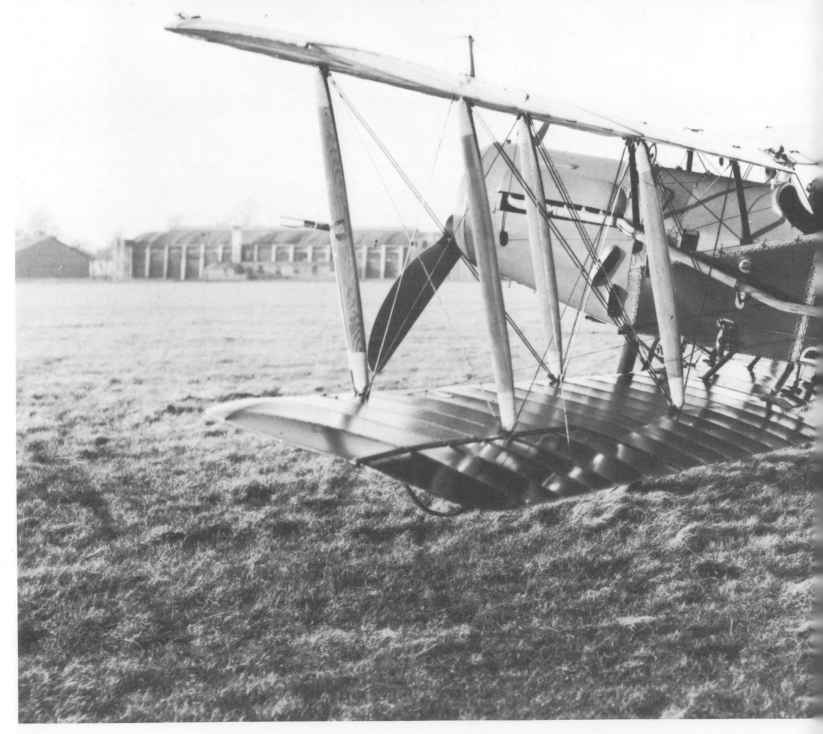

detonator itself contained fulminate of mercury, an extremely sensitive explosive: on impact this was exploded by the striker, setting off an exploder charge of less sensitive material which in turn detonated the main charge of relatively stable TNT or Amatol. By placing the arming propeller on the nose, the striker could be made to initiate the sequence immediately the bomb impacted, an arrangement normally used for antipersonnel fragmentation bombs. Alternatively, by positioning the arming mechanism in the tail, a delay between impact and detonation could be contrived, so that the bomb would bury itself in the ground before exploding, producing a deep crater and representing a more useful method for attacking buildings etc. By 1918 a variety of bombs were in service, ranging from the 20-lb (9-kg) antipersonnel devices through 40-lb (18-kg) phosphorus incendiaries to 50-lb (23-kg), 112-lb (51-kg), 230-lb (104-kg) and 550-lb (249-kg) weapons. These nominal weights included varying proportions of explosive and casing depending on the purpose for which they were to be used, heavy cases with relatively light charges being the rule for fragmentation weapons, and the reverse applying in the case of demolition bombs, known as aerial mines.

For aiming the bombs, the later stages of the war saw the introduction of the negative lens bombsight for light bombers, and more complicated arrangements for the heavier machines, to allow airspeed, height, and estimated wind speed and drift to be taken into account when sighting the target prior to release.

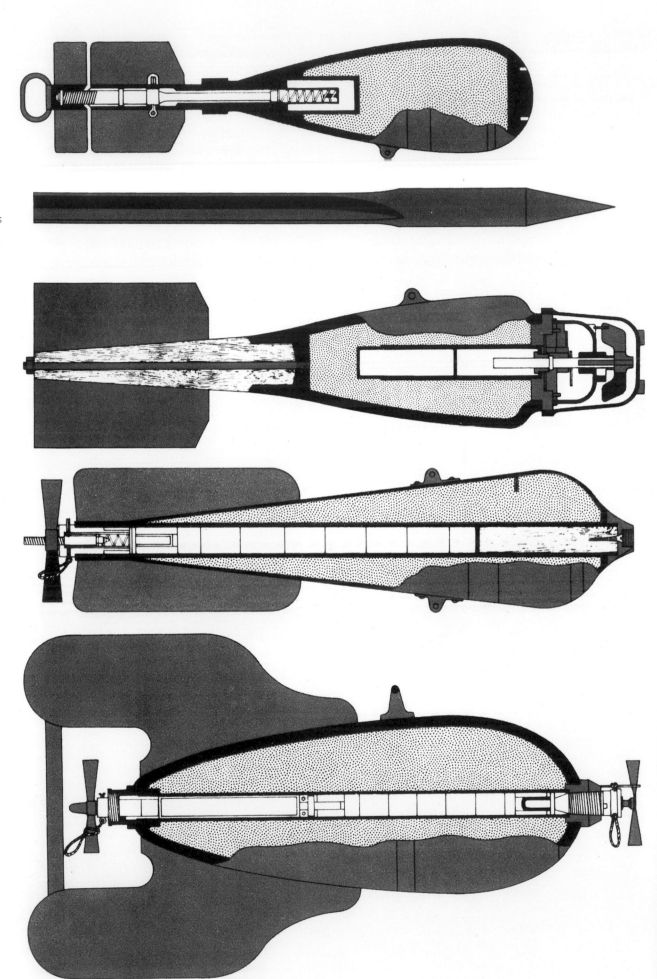

H.E. 'HALE' 20-lb
Designed by Martin Hale in 1913
for the Royal Naval Air Service,
who pioneered British bombing.
Total weight: 18.5lb
Case weight: 14lb
Explosive: 4.5lb Amatol
Case material: steel
Length: 23¼ inches
Diameter: 5 inches
Fuse: tail fuse

**RANKEN ANTI-PERSONNEL
DART (FLECHETTE)**
Made of steel, five inches in length;
dropped from canisters each
containing 500 darts. From 5000ft,
on reaching the ground they
attained the speed of a rifle bullet.

H.E. COOPER 20-lb
Total weight: 24lb
Case weight: 20lb
Explosive: 4lb Amatol
Case material: steel
Length: 24.4 inches
Diamter: 5.1 inches
Fuse: nose fuse
Bomb shown with Safety Cap in
position over nose fuse.

H.E.R.L. 16-lb
Total weight: 16lb
Case weight: 9lb
Explosive: 7lb
Case material: mild steel
Length: 25.15 inches
Diameter: 5 inches
Fuse: tail fuse.

H.E.R.L. 112lb
Total weight: 106lb.
Case weight: 79lb.
Explosive: 28lb.
Case material: Cast steel
Length: 29.1 inches
Diameter: 9 inches.
Fuse: nose or tail fuses.

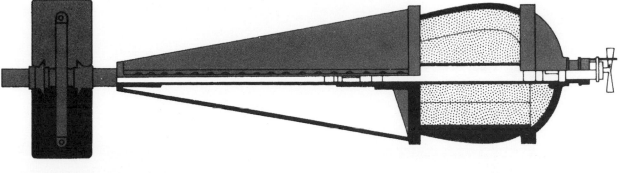

H.E. RAF 336lb.
Total weight: 336lb
Total weight: 336lb.
Case weight: 266lb
Explosive: 70lbs Compressed TNT
Case material: Cast steel
Length: 6ft 9½ inches.
Diameter: 14 inches.
Fuse: nose fuse

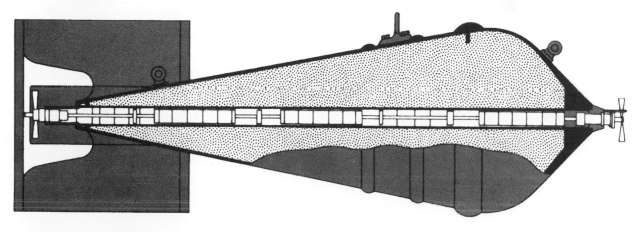

H.E.R.L. 520-lb
(Royal Laboratory Designed)
Total weight: 525lb
Case weight: 180lb
Explosive: 340lb
Case material: steel
Length: 5ft 1 inch
Diameter: 1ft 7½ inches
Fuse: nose and tail fuses.

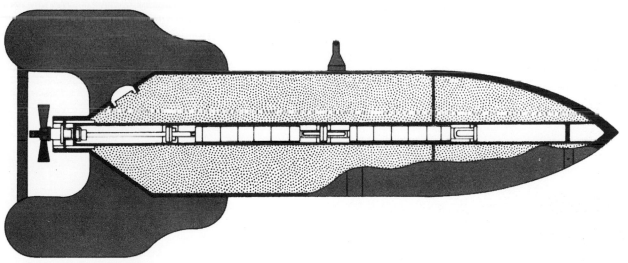

H.E. RFC 230lb
Total weight: 230lb.
Case weight: 90lb.
Explosive: 140lb.
Case material: steel
Length: 50½ inches.
Diameter: 10 inches.
Fuse: tail fuse.

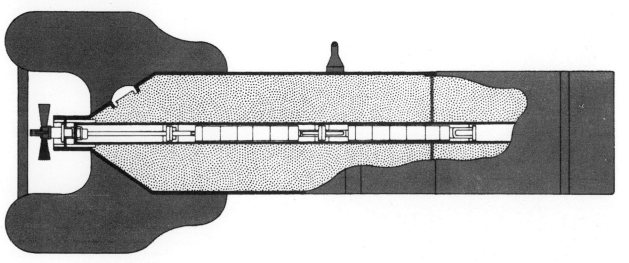

H.E. RFC 230lb.
Flat headed for use at Sea.
Details same as above.

2 OPERATIONS IN 1918

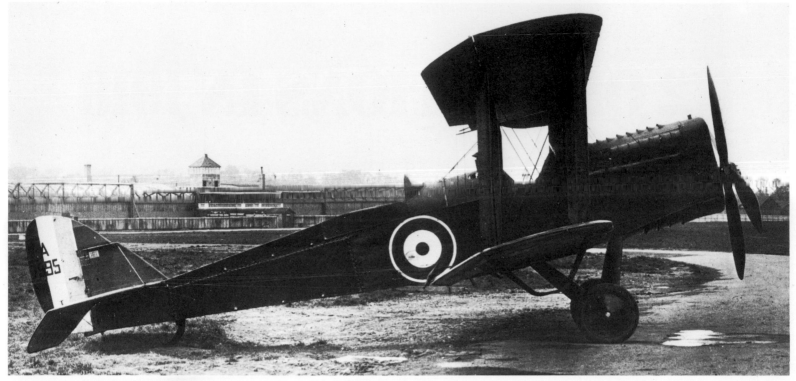

The outstanding Airco D.H.4 equipped No 55 Squadron of the Independent Force, RAF, at its formation in June 1918

The basic equipment of the Royal Air Force squadrons on the Western Front remained unchanged between April 1918 and the Armistice the following November, and the fundamental tasks of reconnaissance, photography and artillery spotting continued. There were, however, new aircraft to come, and new techniques to be developed. At home there was a whole new organisation to be implemented, and overseas operations continued in several theatres.

By the last year of the war, under the stimulus of German raids on Britain and the increasing range and load-carrying ability of the aircraft, there was an increasing emphasis on offensive bombing operations. In October 1917 the 41st Wing, RFC, had been formed with the express intention of carrying out retaliatory raids on Germany. One squadron of D.H.4 day bombers and one each of O/100s and F.E.2bs for night operations made up the new wing, which became VIII Brigade in February 1918. By May a further two squadrons of D.H.9s had been allocated to VIII Brigade, and in the same month it was decided that Trenchard, who had recently resigned as Chief of the Air Staff, should take command of a new bombing formation based at Nancy. Known as the Independent Force, RAF, this came into being on 6 June.

Initially, the Independent Force incorporated the five squadrons of VIII Brigade, whose one squadron of F.E.2bs had been replaced by Handley Page O/400s. But with many new squadrons being formed at home, these were augmented by another three squadrons of O/400s in August, as well as one equipped with the new D.H.9A, and in September a Camel squadron was allocated for escort duties, though the Camel's lack of range made it impossible for these to accompany the bombers on long-distance raids.

The D.H.9A squadron, No 110, was the first to be equipped with the revised version of the disappointing D.H.9, which resulted from the availability of the

major American aeronautical contribution to the war, the 400-hp Liberty engine. Only limited supplies of this new water-cooled V-12 engine were available, and only two squadrons of D.H.9As served in France before the Armistice, but with bigger wings and a redesigned forward fuselage to accommodate the bigger, heavier powerplant, much of the performance lost in the transition from D.H.4 to D.H.9 was restored, and a 660-lb (299-kg) maximum bombload could now be carried at 17,000 ft (5182 m) on unescorted daylight raids.

A pair of Liberty engines powered another de Havilland design for Airco, the D.H.10A Amiens III, which was flown for the first time in the spring of 1918. Like the D.H.9, the Amiens carried most of its bombs inside the fuselage, but with the extra power available a greater load could be carried – up to eight 112-lb (51-kg) bombs were dropped in post-war operations – and top speed was a useful 128 mph (206 km/h) at 6500 ft (1981 m). The dangers of day bombing were reflected in the provision of mountings for single or twin Lewis guns in both nose and dorsal positions, but No 104 Squadron was still in the process of re-equipping with the type when the Armistice intervened to prevent its being used operationally on the Western Front.

With the limited resources at its disposal the Independent Force was never in a position to carry out its ultimate ambition of bombing Germany into submission. Nor, indeed, did its status match its name, since it was under the ultimate control of the Allied command in France as well as being responsible to the Air Council, so that attacks on tactical targets such as railway junctions in support of ground offensives were added to its strategic operations against Germany.

In an account of Independent Force operations, Trenchard quoted a total of 550 tons (558,800 kg) of bombs dropped, 390 tons of which were delivered by

Previous page: French officers visit the RAF airfield at Poix, in the Somme area

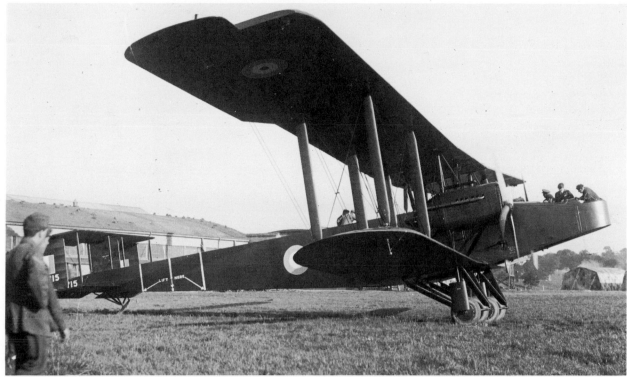

night, and with German airfields being on the receiving end of no less than two-fifths of the total. A further 41 German towns and cities were listed among the targets bombed, but the fighter opposition encountered on daylight raids, which were often subject to continuous attack from the moment they crossed the lines to the moment they returned, meant that losses were inevitably high.

The situation was made worse by autumn weather conditions, so that in September and October many raids were unable to reach their targets, and many aircraft were lost in crashes behind the Allied lines. In fact, no less than 243 of the 352 aircraft lost were listed as wrecked, as opposed to missing behind enemy lines, the majority of which were day bombers. In terms of casualties, too, the day bombing units were the worst sufferers, with most of the 29 killed, 235 missing and 64 wounded being de Havilland crews.

Meanwhile, plans were under way for adding a new dimension to Independent Force operations. In May 1918 the first flight was made of a massive new bomber, the Handley Page V/1500, powered by four 375-hp Rolls-Royce Eagle VIII engines and intended to carry its crew of six and up to 30 250-lb (113-kg) bombs all the way to Berlin from bases in England. Two squadrons, Nos 166 and 167, were formed in June and November respectively to operate the new bomber, and a new 3360-lb (1524-kg) bomb, too big to be carried by anything but the V/1500, was developed in succession to the 1650-lb (748-kg) weapons produced for the earlier Handley Page bombers. The bigger bombs were carried externally, but like the earlier O/100 and O/400 the V/1500 carried bombs of up to 250-lb (113-kg) internally, to be released through spring-loaded doors in the bottom of the fuselage.

As well as its formidable bombload, the V/1500

The Handley Page O/100, originally designed for the RNAS, was the first useful heavy night bomber, and was later improved to produce the O/400

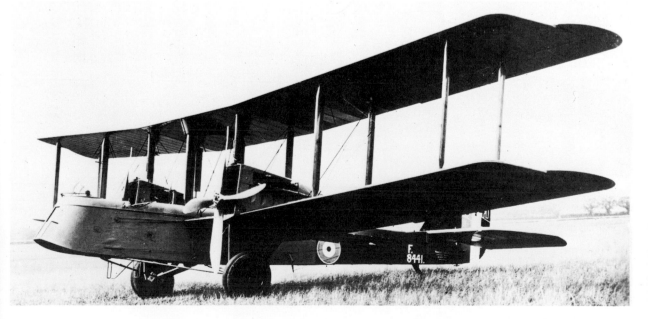

The Airco D.H.10 Amiens in its Mk IIIA form, with the engines moved down to rest on the lower wings. The Amiens was faster and carried a bigger bombload than the D.H.9A, but appeared too late for wartime service

introduced another innovation in the weight of defensive armament carried. The plans for its use included a scheme to establish a base in Prague to which the V/1500s would fly after attacking Berlin, and a system was envisaged whereby the bombers would make round trips between their base at Bircham Newton, in Norfolk, and Prague, bombing Berlin on the outward journey and Essen or Düsseldorf on the return leg. Alternatively, they could fly from Prague to their French bases near Nancy by way of Regensburg or Munich. For protection on such long flights the V/1500 was provided with a total of four gunners' positions, one in the nose, one for upward and downward firing guns just aft of the wings, and a fourth in the tail, which was reached by means of a catwalk.

In the event, No 166 Squadron was preparing for its first raid on Berlin with the first three operational V/1500s when the Armistice put a stop to the plans. At the same time another new night bomber, the Vickers Vimy, was on the point of entering service. The first example of this twin-engined three-seater had reached the Independent Force in France by early November, too late to see action. With the 360-hp Eagle VIII engine the Vimy IV was capable of lifting a total of over 4000 lb (1814 kg) of bombs, and with a lighter load it had an endurance of 11 hours.

Meanwhile, the build-up of RAF strength continued, without quite reaching the target of 200 squadrons set the previous year. Apart from the four new Independent Force squadrons, other new arrivals in France between April and November included three squadrons of F.E.2b night bombers in April, May and June; five of D.H.9s between April and July; and one of D.H.9As in September. Fighter strength was also increased by the addition of a squadron each of Dolphins and F.2Bs in April, three further S.E.5a squadrons between May and October and another Bristol Fighter unit five days before the Armistice.

Among the most interesting of the new arrivals, however, were the two final Camel squadrons, Nos 151 and 152, which transferred to France in June and October respectively. The reason behind the Independent Force's concentration on bombing enemy airfields was the need to prevent German raids on its own bases. The Camels of No 151 Squadron added to this effort by undertaking night intruder missions, waiting in the vicinity of German airfields to attack the bombers as they returned from their missions. Operations began on 27 June, the first success coming a month later and a further 20 victories following before the Armistice intervened.

Another increasingly important area of operations during 1918 was supporting ground troops as the final German offensive was halted and the Allied advances gathered momentum. At least one Camel squadron was allocated to low-level co-operation with armoured forces, supporting the work of the tanks on the ground, and in Britain during the last months of the war four squadrons were busy equipping with a

new aircraft specifically designed for ground-attack work.

The Sopwith T.F.2 Salamander followed the conversion of a Camel as a 'trench fighter', the latter having an armoured cockpit floor and two Lewis guns firing downwards through the bottom of the cockpit, plus a third mounted above the upper wing. Both this and the Salamander were designed after standard fighters had suffered very high casualties in ground-strafing operations, and since low-flying aircraft were particularly vulnerable to small-arms fire from the ground the new machine incorporated no less than 650 lb (295 kg) of armour enclosing the forward part of the fuselage to protect the cockpit, engine and fuel tank. Armament was the standard pair of synchronised Vickers guns, which were provided with 1000 rounds of ammunition each, and four 20-lb (9-kg) bombs could be carried under the fuselage. However, the fighting ended before the Salamander could be tried in action.

The Salamander was largely derived from another

Above: Aircrew of No 216 Squadron, VIII Brigade, in front of one of their O/400s at their base at Cramaille, near Amiens, in April 1918

Left: The Vickers Vimy heavy night bomber appeared too late for wartime operations, but saw post-war service with several RAF squadrons

new Sopwith fighter which did see service in France. This was the Snipe, which followed the Camel in using a nine-cylinder rotary engine, the 230-hp Bentley B.R.2, and proved to have a better rate of climb than its predecessor. It also offered a high degree of manoeuvrability without the Camel's associated difficulty of handling. Deliveries to squadrons began in the summer of 1918, but only three squadrons on the Western Front were flying Snipes before the Armistice, and a long-range variant intended for use as an escort with the Independent Force arrived too late.

While operations in France continued to increase in scope and intensity, the German air raids on Britain which had provoked the amalgamation of the RFC and RNAS had been met by the formation of a number of home defence squadrons. In April 1918 there were five of these, based along the east coast from Kent to the Firth of Forth, and using a variety of aircraft, including some, such as the Sopwith Pup and 1½-Strutter, which had been withdrawn from the fighting in France. There were also Camels, S.E.5as and Avro 504Ks, the last being one of a series of variants on a design dating back to 1913, and whose J model had been the first purpose-designed military trainer.

In fact, by this stage the German strategic air offensive was virtually over, though sporadic raids were enough to ensure that anti-aircraft batteries and the home defence squadrons were maintained. The last airship raid on northern England took place on 12 April, following which a new command was formed for air defence of the north.

During the spring of 1918 the German bombers had been diverted to the support of the offensive on the Western Front, but on 19 May a force of 43 bombers took off to carry out the biggest and, as it turned out, last attack on London. By this stage the communications system on the ground and night-flying techniques in the air had improved to the extent that three of the raiders were shot down by RAF fighters and another three fell victim to ground fire. Less than half

the bombers reached London, and the demands from the Western Front prevented any more raids by the bombers. Only one more airship raid followed, on 5 August. This was directed against the Midlands, but the resulting destruction of one of the latest Zeppelins finally ended such operations.

Another reorganisation involved the coastal patrol flights based at RNAS stations around the coast of Great Britain. As part of the RNAS these had been organised as stations operating both seaplanes and landplanes, but in August they were allocated squadron numbers, separate units being formed for the two kinds of aircraft. A total of 20 seaplane squadrons were formed at 16 stations, while another 14 squadrons of landplanes operated from 13 bases, three of which were associated with seaplane establishments. In addition, No 219 Squadron at Westgate, in Kent, No 253 on the Isle of Wight and No 246 at Seaton Carew, in County Durham, had both seaplane and landplane flights. No 230 Squadron at Felixstowe and No 233 at Dover, as well as No 219, also operated Camels as escorts for the maritime patrols off the southeast coast, while across the Channel at Cherbourg and Oudelzee, near Dunkirk, were another two seaplane squadrons engaged in similar duties.

The most common type of floatplane with these squadrons was the Short 184, sole equipment of seven squadrons and in service with another eight. The 184 had pioneered the launching of torpedoes from aircraft, and was used to carry bombs of up to 520 lb (236 kg) in weight, though performance with a torpedo under its fuselage was marginal at best. The diminutive Sopwith Baby, another twin-float seaplane, was still in service with five squadrons, and while the Short 184 used various engines ranging from 230 to 300 hp the Baby's standard powerplant was a 130-hp Clerget rotary, and when armed with a Lewis gun it could carry no more than a single 65-lb (29-kg) bomb.

Also used in considerable numbers were the Felixstowe F.2A and F.3 flying boats. These originated as Curtiss flying boats redesigned by Squadron Commander John C Porte of the RNAS station at Felixstowe. Powered by a pair of Rolls-Royce Eagle engines, the F.2A entered service in 1917 and in August 1918 was used by nine of the coastal patrol squadrons. Although not particularly fast or manoeuvrable, it was armed with at least four and as many as seven Lewis guns, could carry two 230-lb (104-kg) bombs and had an endurance of six hours, qualities which made it an excellent maritime patrol type.

The German U-Boat campaign constituted one of the most serious threats to Britain's survival during the First World War. Between February and July 1917 shipping losses had amounted to 2,350,000 tons (2,387,600,000 kg), plus a further 1,500,000 tons of Allied and neutral shipping. The eventual introduction of the convoy system for merchant shipping across the Atlantic and through the Mediterranean finally succeeded in turning the tide against the U-Boats on the high seas, but a vital contribution to this success came from the measures adopted to stop the U-Boats reaching the Atlantic through the Straits of Dover, and to restrict their mine-laying and other activities in the North Sea.

Among these measures were aircraft patrols to supplement those of the surface ships. By the end of 1917 more than 60 per cent of ships lost were sunk within 10 miles of the shore, and in March 1918 a scheme of protected shipping lanes was adopted. The idea was that these should be patrolled every 20 minutes by aircraft, and it was not considered necessary to sink U-Boats: as long as they were aware of the threat they would be reluctant to surface or use their periscopes to look for targets. On standard patrols aircraft would normally fly at a height of 1000 ft (305 m), though when actually escorting convoys altitude would be reduced to around 600 ft (183 m) to improve their view of the surface while keeping the whole of the danger zone under observation.

Although the F.2A was not the handiest of aircraft as far as speed and manoeuvrability were concerned, it proved able to hold its own against the opposition from German seaplanes over the Channel. On one occasion, on 4 June 1914, three F.2As successfully defended another which had been forced down with a broken fuel line against an attacking force of 14 German aircraft, shooting down no less than six of the enemy machines. Unfortunately, the F.3 which succeeded the F.2A in production proved slower and more sluggish than the earlier model, though able to carry a bigger bombload over longer distances.

The last of the Felixstowe flying boats to enter production, the F.5, was delayed by the decision to use substantial amounts of F.3 components in its construction. As a result, the first examples did not enter service until November, too late to see active service before the war ended. Another new seaplane which arrived too late to have much impact was the Fairey IIIB, a single-engined twin-float variant of the

The Felixstowe F.3, successor to the F.2A, one of the principal types of flying boat used for coastal patrols during 1918

IIIA using the same 260-hp Sunbeam Maori engine and able to carry two 230-lb (104-kg) bombs. Only 25 were produced, and these entered service with three squadrons in October and November.

Primary equipment of the landplane coastal patrol squadrons was the D.H.6, originally produced in 1917 as a trainer. To this end it was designed to have a very low landing speed and be impossible to stall, but in the process it developed a number of unfortunate handling qualities and was replaced in the training role by the Avro 504. In the meantime, large numbers had been built, and early in 1918 many of these were allocated to coastal patrol flights. For this work they were flown as single-seaters carrying a 100-lb (45-kg) bomb.

D.H.4s, D.H.9s, D.H.9As and B.E.2cs were also used in small numbers during 1918, and No 246 Squadron also operated the Blackburn Kangaroo. The Kangaroo's twin engines enabled it to carry a much heavier bombload than the D.H.6, and on 28 August one of the 10 in service inflicted severe damage on *UC-70* when scoring a near miss with a 520-lb (236-kg) bomb. The submarine was subsequently destroyed by depth charges from the destroyer HMS *Ouse*.

During the war considerable progress was made in launching aircraft from ships. Converted merchant ships were equipped to carry floatplanes, which had to be hoisted in and out of the water before they could take off; Sopwith Camels were flown from platforms on gun turrets aboard capital ships; and successful experiments were carried out with aircraft launched from barges towed behind ships. By October 1918 the first true aircraft carrier, HMS *Argus* was in service, and in that month No 185 Squadron was formed to operate the Sopwith Cuckoo torpedo bombers with which it was planned that *Argus* would launch an attack on the German High Sea Fleet. With a 200-hp Sunbeam Arab engine the Cuckoo had a top speed of just over 100 mph (161 km/h), and proved suitably stable for launching the 1000-lb (454-kg) torpedo it was built to carry, though the powerplant was a constant source of trouble and the war was over before any attack could be carried out.

Another experimental technique tested in the summer of 1918 involved the release of a Camel from the airship *R.33*. The idea was to provide the airship with her own aeroplane escort which could be released in the event of an attack by hostile aircraft. Two successful launches were made, the Camel gliding safely to the ground on the first occasion, and starting its engines and carrying out a powered landing on the second, but further experiments along these lines had to wait until after the war.

While Britain and the Western Front were the main areas of RAF activity during 1918, many units served in other theatres. Following the rout of the Italian army by the Austrians at Caporetto and the retreat to the Piave river in October 1917, reinforcements were sent to northern Italy from the Western Front. Among these were three Camel squadrons and one of R.E.8s. One flight of the latter formed the basis

for a new Bristol Fighter squadron in July, and one of the Camel units returned to France to join the Independent Force in September, but the remainder continued to fight on the Piave front until the Austrian surrender at the beginning of November.

In southern Italy the RNAS units around Taranto and Otranto were organised into RAF squadrons in April. Three of these were bomber squadrons using D.H.4s and D.H.9s, the fourth being a Camel squadron used to escort the bombers on raids against Austrian bases in Albania and Montenegro, on the other side of the Adriatic. Antisubmarine patrols were also flown in support of the Otranto barrage, a somewhat ineffectual attempt to prevent Austrian submarines passing through the Straits of Otranto into the Mediterranean. They were joined in this work in September by two new seaplane squadrons flying a

mixture of Short 184s and the more powerful Type 320 derivative, Sopwith Babys and Felixstowe F.3s.

Other RNAS units in the Mediterranean and Aegean were also formed into RAF squadrons for antisubmarine work using similar assortments of seaplanes. One was based at Gibraltar and two on the island of Malta, and another at Suda Bay, Crete, with a detachment on Siros, while a fourth divided its flights between the islands of Limnos and Skyros, in the northern Aegean. In October another two antisubmarine squadrons were formed from the RNAS seaplane flights at Port Said and Alexandria, in Egypt.

In Macedonia, meanwhile, a substantial Allied force facing the Bulgarian army which had occupied Serbia was supported by several British squadrons. After 1 April these included three former RNAS units, two equipped with D.H.4 and D.H.9 bombers and the

Above: Starting the 400-hp US-built Liberty engine of a D.H.9A. The new powerplant transformed the disappointing D.H.9, and the revised design became a standard RAF general purpose aircraft during the 1920s

Left: The Blackburn Kangaroo served as a coastal patrol aircraft during 1918: 11 of the 12 U-Boats sighted by Kangaroos were attacked, and one was damaged before being finished off by a destroyer

35

other with Camels, based at Stavros and on the islands of Thasos and Lesbos. The ex-RFC squadrons comprised two of mixed bomber-reconnaissance types, mainly F.K.8s, and another formed on 1 April to take over the fighter elements of the other two. Again, these included a mixture of types, among them S.E.5as, Nieuport 17s and Camels, as well as the unusual Bristol M.1C, the only monoplane fighter to serve with the RAF during the war.

Monoplanes had been the subject of an official ban imposed in 1912 after a series of crashes, and although this only lasted until February 1913 single-wing fighters were largely ignored by British designers for many years afterwards. A rare exception was the Bristol M.1A of 1916, and after this had demonstrated a speed of 132 mph (213 km/h) with a 110-hp Clerget engine four armed M.1Bs were built. One of these was tested in France in January 1917, but despite an enthusiastic reception from the pilots who flew it Trenchard's suggestion that further examples might be given to the Russians marked the end of its career on the Western Front. However, after the other three

M.1Bs had been tested, 125 of the M.1C version, armed with a single synchronised Vickers gun in the nose, were produced, though only 32 of these found their way to front-line squadrons in the Middle East.

On the front with Bulgaria there was stalemate until September 1918, when a successful offensive was launched. As the Bulgarian columns retreated through mountain ravines they were attacked repeatedly by aircraft. This action was instrumental in ending the fighting in the region, the Bulgarians declining to join the Germans in continuing the war, and by the end of the month Bulgarian opposition was at an end, opening the way for an advance on Constantinople.

The main base for British operations in the Middle East was Egypt, though by 1918 the battle against the Turkish forces had moved away from the Suez Canal and Sinai peninsula into Palestine. In April there were three army co-operation squadrons flying mainly R.E.8s and one fighter squadron with S.E.5as, as well as No 1 Squadron of the Australian Flying Corps, supporting Allenby's forces in the drive towards Syria. These were reinforced in August and September by

Standard trainer during 1918, the Avro 504K was built in greater numbers than any other British aircraft of the First World War

new squadrons formed in Egypt a few months earlier, one using D.H.9s and the other S.E.5as.

One important contribution made by the aircraft in this theatre was the aerial mapping of the terrain. They had also been able to establish air superiority towards the end of 1917, denying the Turkish forces and their German commanders the benefits of aerial reconnaissance and paving the way for Allenby's occupation of Jerusalem in December 1917. By September 1918 Allenby was ready to move against the Turkish positions in Syria, entering Damascus on 2 October, two days after Bulgaria's surrender, and with Constantinople now threatened from both sides the Turks were left with no option but to ask for an armistice, which was duly signed on 30 October.

The farthest-flung of all the RAF squadrons in 1918 were two based in the North-West Frontier region of India. Stationed at Lahore and Risalpur, these flew B.E.2cs and B.E.2es for army co-operation tasks.

Obviously, such a large and widespread distribution of operational units could not be sustained without a massive training and maintenance establishment.

It has been calculated that 17 people were needed to keep a single training aircraft serviceable, and for front-line aircraft this figure rose to 47. After the creation of the Royal Air Force a large recruitment of civilians became necessary to replace the aircrew who had previously been drawn mainly from within the army and transferred to the RFC.

By 1918 training had been organised on a large scale and was carried out on a systematic basis. After undergoing basic training, potential aircrew spent two months as cadets at one of the eight Schools of Aeronautics, where they received instruction on the theory of flight and such subjects as aircraft rigging, engines and armament, map-reading and photography. After graduating as probationary second lieutenants (between April 1918 and August of the following year, RAF ranks corresponded to the army ranks as used by the RFC), they were posted to one of the 70 Training Depot Stations, where training squadrons were based.

Pilot training was based on the use of dual-control Avro 504Ks, which by the end of the year were being delivered at the rate of 80 a week. The 504 had been selected for the task because of its flying qualities: being fully aerobatic, it enabled pupils to experience the full possibilities of flying, whereas the earlier idea of using slow, stable trainers had left pilots ill-prepared for the transfer to combat types. The underlying philosophy was that the trainee pilots should fly from the pilot's seat from the beginning and should learn how to control the aircraft in any situation – in other words, they should be taught to recover from any awkward situation they might find themselves in, rather than being taught to avoid dangerous manoeuvres, in the belief that confidence in their own ability would be their greatest asset in combat. Pilot instructors by this stage were specially trained at one of the five instructors' schools, according to the methods laid down by Major R R Smith-Barry, who had devised the whole system.

Following basic flying training, pilots underwent specialist training at one of the five fighter, four bomber or one army co-operation schools. These were not all in Britain: a large training establishment had been built up in Egypt, and by 1918 this included six of the Training Depot Stations along with a school of aeronautics and one each of the specialist training schools for fighter and bomber pilots. Aircraft were also assembled in Egypt: by the end of 1918 20 of the 504Ks delivered each week were in kit form for assembly at the Eastern Aircraft Factory at Aboukir.

Further training was undertaken in North America. A Training Brigade in Canada included 15 training squadrons at three camps, as well as a school for fighter pilots. Under an agreement with the United States, winter training was carried out in Texas, in return for American pilots being trained in Canada during the summer, and during 1918 this system was providing 200 pilots a month, while American participation in the war also resulted in the provision of thousands of mechanics.

3 COLONIAL PEACE-KEEPING, 1919-25

The end of the war in Europe brought an end to many plans, among them that of building 255 V/1500s to bomb Berlin. Within a month of the Armistice, however, the third prototype of the giant Handley Page bomber was being prepared for an even more ambitious journey: Major Stuart Maclaren and Captain Robert Halley were to fly the aircraft to Delhi, carrying as passenger the new Air Officer Commanding, India, General Norman MacEwen.

After one false start, when the reduction gear in one of the engines seized up within 15 minutes of take-off, the expedition, including two fitters and a rigger to look after maintenance, left Martlesham Heath, Suffolk, on 13 December 1918. The first leg of the journey, planned to reach Paris, was disrupted by low cloud, but at least took them across the Channel to Bergues, near Dunkirk, lately the base for D.H.4s and Camels. Le Bourget, Paris, was reached on the next stage, and the weather continued to cause delays and route changes. Beaune, Pisa and Catania, Sicily, replaced Marseilles, Rome and Otranto as the next three stops: at Catania the big aeroplane became bogged down on landing, and a night take-off from the racecourse on Malta was aided by the demolition of a wall to extend the run.

The next landing was in the Western Desert of Egypt after the reduction gears of two engines seized up, but help was summoned, and while the officers travelled to Cairo by rail, the mechanics repaired the aircraft, which was then flown to Cairo. Leaving Cairo on 8 January 1919, the expedition reached Baghdad on the following day, and after three days spent on repairs to the propellers further stops were made at Bushire and Bundar Abbas, with only one emergency landing at Ahwaz, before another engine failure led to another forced landing, this time on a spit of wet sand at Ormara on the coast of Baluchistan. A fortunate change of wind allowed them to take off, however, and they struggled on, reaching Karachi with only one engine each side still going and landing with the help of an improvised flarepath on 15 January.

This epic flight had been made in the most difficult circumstances. Apart from constant attention to aeroplane and engines, the mechanics were faced with the task of emptying 250 four-gallon cans of petrol through chamois leather filters into the fuel tanks at every stop. There was clearly room for improvement in both the reliability of aircraft and the facilities for long-distance flights, and as it turned out this was to be one of the RAF's major areas of expansion in the subsequent decade.

At home, the vast organisation that had been built up during the war was being dismantled. A few squadrons went to Germany with the occupation forces, though by the end of the year only No 12's Bristol Fighters remained. Some isolated units had become embroiled in the civil war in Russia, and three squadrons were in Ireland on army co-operation duties. The other squadrons on the Western Front were brought home or disbanded. Winston Churchill became joint Secretary of State for both War and Air and the Admiralty was agitating for the return of the naval air arm. The prospects looked bleak for a separate air force.

Against this background Sykes, whose proposals for the post-war period were rejected as too expensive – originally these centred on the creation of an Imperial Air Force incorporating Canadian, Australian, South African and New Zealand elements and a chain of flying boat bases around the world, later reduced to a 62-squadron home air force – was moved from his post as Chief of the Air Staff and given responsibility for civil aviation. Trenchard, who had been dismayed by what he considered the unnecessary duplication of effort involved in the creation of the Independent Force, was then invited by Churchill to submit his ideas. These involved an altogether more modest force, and confirmed Churchill's resolve to have Trenchard as the new CAS in place of Sykes.

In his new capacity Trenchard was responsible for a White Paper published in December 1919 entitled *Permanent Organisation of the Air Force*. This assumed that there would be no European war for some years, and that the immediate requirement was for the minimum force necessary to garrison overseas bases. These were seen as potential replacements for at least some of the conventional military forces overseas on the grounds that they would be cheaper to maintain and quicker to react in an emergency.

The specific recommendations were for seven squadrons in Egypt, three in Iraq and eight in India, the last to be paid for by the colonial government. A

small reserve force should be maintained in Egypt, 'the Clapham Junction of the air', as it was termed, along with a seaplane unit at Alexandria and another on Malta. The home air force meanwhile would be reduced to the bare minimum of four land and two seaplane squadrons, apart from three for naval duties and two for army co-operation. These were regarded as constituting the foundation for any expansion that might be necessary in the future.

At the same time, training was regarded as being of fundamental importance. A college at Cranwell in Lincolnshire was to be opened to train officer cadets, while boys would be recruited and trained as apprentices at Halton, in Hertfordshire, for the technical trades, or at Uxbridge, Middlesex. The third aspect of Trenchard's scheme was research, and the Royal Aircraft Establishment, as the former Royal Aircraft Factory at Farnborough had been renamed the previous year, and the Aircraft and Armament Experimental Establishment at Martlesham Heath, Suffolk, were to be retained.

The publication of the White Paper came at the end of a year which had seen not only a great deal of debate about the future of the RAF, but also one demonstration of the potential for its use. Afghanistan, on the northwestern frontier of India, had seen three wars involving the British army during the 19th century, and in 1919 trouble flared again when the frontier tribes began carrying out attacks across the border. Even with the aid of reinforcements from Iraq the Indian Army was finding it difficult to contain the uprising.

The V/1500 which had made the trip from England, meanwhile, had been repaired and fitted with new engines at Karachi before being flown to an official reception at Delhi, and by March it had arrived at Lahore, where it was to be dismantled. However, when plans to use an O/400 which Captain Ross Smith had flown to India from Palestine in July 1918 were thwarted by the destruction of the aircraft in a dust storm at the frontier air station of Risalpur early in May, it was decided to repair the V/1500 and use it instead for a bombing raid on the Afghan capital of Kabul.

This was a tall order. The V/1500 had suffered a series of forced landings on its journey from England, and had been subject to several months of extremely hot weather following its arrival, and to reach Kabul it would have to negotiate the Jagdalak Pass, nearly 8000 ft (2438 m) above sea level. Nevertheless, the aeroplane was repaired successfully and fitted with racks for four 112-lb (51-kg) bombs. Another 16 20-lb (9-kg) bombs were carried in the cockpit, from which they were to be dropped through a door in the floor by Lieutenant Ted Villiers, acting as bomb-aimer/navigator, and who made up the crew along with the three NCOs who had made the journey from England and who had been responsible for restoring the aircraft. The pilot was Captain Halley.

Having attained an encouraging 6700 ft (2042 m) on a test flight, the V/1500 was prepared for the raid, taking off in the early hours of 24 May. It took an hour to reach the 3000 ft (914 m) altitude needed to cross the Khyber Pass, and despite a leak in the cooling

The massive Handley Page V/1500, planned to be able to bomb Berlin in 1918, dropped its only bombs in anger over Kabul in May of the following year

The D.H.9 ambulance that
accompanied the expedition to
British Somaliland, now the
Republic of Somalia, in 1918

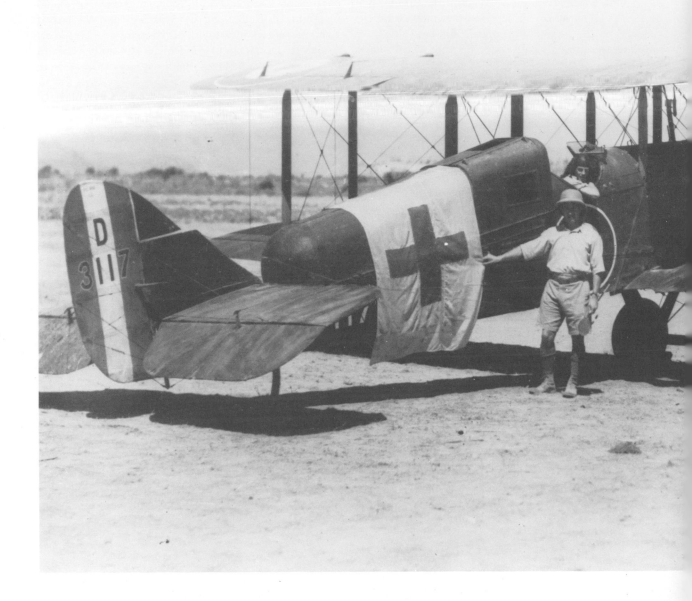

Some of the 12 D.H.9s shipped to
Somalia from Egypt, with sheets of
cardboard protecting the airframes
from the effects of the sun

system the bomber negotiated the Jagdalak Pass with the aid of a following wind and reached Kabul. The return journey, too, was aided by a change in the wind, and despite having to do without the leaking engine for the final stages it returned to Risalpur after a flight lasting six hours.

The effects of the bombs, which reportedly caused damage to a golf course and the royal harem, were probably secondary to the alarm created by the sight of the monstrous bomber: in any case, an immediate settlement was reached with King Amanullah, involving the recognition of Afghanistan's independence and an end to the border conflict. Almost immediately after the White Paper's publication an opportunity was found to test Trenchard's theories in a more realistic fashion than struggling up the Khyber Pass and dropping a few bombs on a defenceless city whose inhabitants had never even seen an aeroplane before.

The protectorate of British Somaliland, in the horn of East Africa, had experienced severe disturbances since the turn of the century as a result of the independence struggles of Sayyid Muhammad and his Dervish followers. These had been forced to withdraw into the interior while the local camel constabulary controlled the coastal area, but during the war one of their forts had been captured and a British naval blockade had curtailed the Dervishes' supply of arms.

A request from the local administration for further action to finish off the rebellion brought the suggestion from Trenchard that a squadron of bombers acting in conjunction with the forces already in the area might save the cost of another military expedition. Despite the opposition of Sir Henry Wilson, Chief of the Imperial General Staff, Trenchard's offer was accepted by the War and Colonial Offices: accordingly, 12 D.H.9s, along with another equipped as a flying ambulance for casualty evacuation and a number of armoured cars and other motor vehicles, were transported from Egypt to Berbera aboard the seaplane carrier *Ark Royal*.

The bombers' job was to destroy the dissidents' strongholds, force them into the open and disperse them with the help of the motorised troops. This was achieved within three weeks of their arrival in January 1920: after his stronghold at Taleh had been destroyed, the Dervish leader fled into the Ogaden, only to be driven out by hostile tribes, and although he then built new forts in Ethiopia, he died before the end of the year, bringing the rebellion to an end.

Meanwhile, there were more weighty problems to be resolved, among them the future of the occupied parts of the former Ottoman empire. Before 1914 this had stretched southeast along the shores of the Red Sea and Persian Gulf, and during the war a series of secret treaties had apportioned the territories among the Allies, while public statements had promised self-determination to the subject nations in return for their help. There were added complications in the form of commercial oil interests in the area, and in the Balfour Declaration of 1917, by which the British Foreign

Secretary had promised British support for the establishment of a Jewish state in Palestine.

At a peace conference in San Remo in April 1920 it was agreed that the French should administer Syria and the Lebanon, while the British would retain Iraq and Palestine, the latter being divided to create a new state east of the Jordan river to be known as Transjordan. Turkey itself was occupied by Allied forces and subject to incursions by the Greeks, leading to a further nationalist uprising under the leadership of Mustafa Kemal. The dismay caused by this settlement in Iraq produced a full-scale war in the summer of 1920, but this was quelled by the arrival of a new High Commissioner in October, and the following March a conference of the British proconsuls in the Middle East and India was held at Cairo.

The Cairo conference was called by Winston Churchill, who by this stage had become Colonial Secretary with responsibility for the Middle East, and it was used to put into effect the system of RAF garrisons proposed by Trenchard. To mollify nationalist sentiment the Emirs Faisal and Abdullah were established as kings of Iraq and Transjordan respectively, although the whole area was to remain under effective British control.

Air Vice-Marshal Sir John Salmond duly became Air Officer Commanding British Forces Iraq in October 1922, with eight squadrons of aircraft and a single infantry brigade to replace 39 battalions of troops. In addition, an armoured car force was formed, and since Sir Henry Wilson's opposition to air control extended to a refusal to allow the army to man these, they were provided by the RAF. In 1925 the RAF's armoured car force, equipped with Lancia and Rolls-Royce vehicles, reached a peak strength of five companies, four in Iraq and one in Transjordan.

Top: Trenchard at Hinaidi in the early 1920s, with Victoria transports and D.H.10 bombers arrayed in the background

Above right: The Rolls-Royce armoured car HMAC Orion, with Vickers gun in the turret

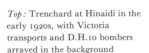

Right: No 1 Armoured Car Company on the move in Iraq in the early 1920s

By this stage the development of aircraft had settled into a pattern it was to follow for several years. The Air Ministry would issue specifications outlining its requirements in particular fields, and interested companies would produce proposals, of which prototypes might be ordered. Following competitive trials, assuming requirements had not changed and satisfactory results had been obtained, half a dozen of the best model would be ordered for development, and after service evaluation production might be ordered. This leisurely approach to aircraft procurement was a consequence of extreme financial stringency, which in turn resulted from the 'Ten-Year Rule'. First promulgated in 1919, this rule stated that all estimates for defence expenditure should be based on the assumption that there would be no major war within 10 years.

As a result, by the end of 1921 the RAF's standard equipment comprised aircraft developed before the end of the war: Avro 504Ks for training, Sopwith Snipe fighters, D.H.9A light bombers, D.H.10 day bombers, Vickers Vimy heavy bombers, Bristol Fighters for army co-operation and F.2A and F.5 flying boats for coastal patrol.

The new style of operations demanded by its role as a colonial peace-keeping force led to some innovations. By 1922 the first Vickers Vernon troop carriers were in service. Developed from the Vimy, the Vernon could accommodate 10 passengers or four stretcher cases loaded through the nose. Performance in desert conditions with the original Eagle engines was somewhat marginal, but with Napier Lion engines the Vernon II showed considerable improvement. Among the Vernon II's duties was the carriage of the Baghdad-Cairo air mail, a regular fortnightly service which helped establish a desert air route between the Egyptian and Iraqi capitals.

Above: The Vickers Virginia Mk X, standard heavy bomber of the late 1920s and early 1930s, carried a crew of four and up to 3000 lb (1361 kg) of bombs

Above right: The Fairey Fawn was designed as a replacement for the D.H.9A, but proved to have inferior performance and only served with three squadrons in the mid-1920s

Right: Vickers Victoria Mk VI bomber transports. This troop-carrying version of the Virginia was used by two squadrons in Iraq for more than 10 years from 1926

The original mainstay of the desert air mail service, and one of the main workhorses of the RAF in the Middle East during the 1920s was the D.H.9A. For desert conditions the D.H.9A was equipped with an extra radiator, thorn-proof tyres and an auxiliary fuel tank under the upper starboard wing. A spare wheel was normally carried on the fuselage, while the internal load would include emergency rations and water, and with the frequent addition of tents and bedding carried externally both appearance and performance deteriorated. Nevertheless, the type continued to serve the desert force throughout the decade.

The successors of the Vimy and Vernon also came from Vickers in the form of the Virginia bomber and its transport derivative, the Victoria. The former was produced in a number of models, all of which used Napier Lion engines, and the majority of which were all-metal Mk Xs carrying a crew of four and a 3000-lb (1361-kg) bombload. Three home-based squadrons used the type during the 1920s, though several more squadrons were equipped with Virginias when they reformed in the 1930s.

The Virginia's troop-carrying counterpart, the Victoria, served with Nos 70 and 216 squadrons at Hinaidi, the main RAF base in Iraq, from 1926 until the mid-1930s. A maximum of 20 passengers could be carried by the Victoria, which was also equipped for a bombload of 1000 lb (454 kg). The aiming arrangement used for the Victoria's bombs was one developed on its predecessor, the Vernon, involving a panel in the cockpit floor through which the target was sighted.

Another heavy bomber of this period, the Avro Aldershot, was unusual in having only a single engine. With its 650-hp Rolls-Royce Condor, the Aldershot was still able to carry a 2000-lb (907-kg) bombload, but it served with only one squadron from 1924–26, as it was decided that heavy bombers should have two engines. A derivative of the Aldershot known as the Andover was planned to take over the desert air mail, but in the event only four were built, and these were used for ambulance and transport work in Britain.

The replacement for the Aldershot with No 99 Squadron was the Handley Page Hyderabad, which, despite its twin Lion engines, carried a bombload of only 1100 lb (499 kg) in addition to its crew of four. In fact, the most noteworthy aspect of the Hyderabad was its place as the RAF's last wooden biplane bomber. It represented very little improvement over the Independent Force's equipment of 1918, having been developed from a civil airliner of 1919.

Further evidence of lack of progress in aircraft development was provided by the Fairey Fawn, designed as a replacement for the D.H.9A and first flown in 1922, but which proved to have inferior performance to the earlier type. Three squadrons used the Fawn for two years from 1924, all of them based in England. The other two D.H.9A squadrons in Britain, and all those abroad, continued to use the older machines until newer types appeared later in the decade. By 1925 there were eight D.H.9A squadrons overseas, comprising two in India, four in Iraq, one in Palestine and Transjordan and another in Egypt.

The continuing debate on the role of the air force led to the setting up of the Salisbury committee when Bonar Law became prime minister in 1923. The new committee was appointed to consider the relationship between the three services and the strength needed for the RAF to maintain its defensive role.

The committee's initial report, accepted by the Cabinet despite Bonar Law's initial inclination to return the RAF to Army and Navy control, recommended the retention of an independent air force and a strength of 52 squadrons for home defence. The French air force was the yardstick by which the necessary strength was measured, the general principle being that the home defence force should be strong enough to provide protection against an attack by the strongest air force within striking distance. Furthermore, this expansion, amounting to a trebling of the number of squadrons then in existence, was to be accomplished within five years, and 13 of the new squadrons were to be reserve or auxiliary units.

However, Trenchard's idea of a defensive air force was one composed mainly of bombers, capable of destroying an enemy's sources of supply and the morale of its people. He regarded the destruction of individual bombers as a waste of time when the factory producing them could be destroyed instead, and believed the latter end to be attainable by unescorted bombers, many of which would have to carry out daylight attacks to achieve the necessary degree of accuracy. Fighters, therefore, were to be kept to the minimum number of short-range interceptors.

The result was that new fighters were just as scarce as new bombers, though they were considerably more attractive. The Snipe continued to be the principal fighter during the early 1920s. Three of the four squadrons in existence in 1920 – one in Britain, two in India and one in Egypt – were redeployed during the next two years, the Egyptian and one of the Indian squadrons disbanding, the other moving to Hinaidi. Subsequently new Snipe squadrons were formed at home bases in accordance with the expanding home defence requirements: one in November 1922, four in April 1923, and two more in each of the next two years.

By this stage, however, replacement of the Snipe was already under way, and the first of the new fighters, the Gloster Grebe, entered service with a single flight of another new squadron, No 111, in October 1923. The Grebe was notable for its use of the High Lift Biplane combination of a high-lift upper wing with a medium-lift, low-drag lower wing developed by Gloster designer Henry Folland, giving higher efficiency at cruising speeds and allowing a reduction in wing area. Otherwise, with its radial engine – in this case the 325-hp, nine-cylinder Armstrong Siddeley Jaguar III – and twin Vickers guns in the nose, it was typical of British fighters of the period. After evaluation by No 111, the Grebe II with 400-hp Jaguar IV was ordered, and five squadrons were equipped with the type between September 1924 and January 1925.

The Jaguar engine was also used in the Armstrong Whitworth Siskin, developed from a 1918 design, but in its Mk III version using a fabric-covered metal fuselage and wings. The 54 ordered entered service

The first new fighter to enter RAF service after 1918, the Gloster Grebe was a favourite aerobatic aircraft

with Nos 41 and 111 Squadrons in May and June 1924 as the RAF's first all-steel fighters.

Whereas the Grebe and the Siskin represented the fruits of prolonged private development by their respective manufacturers, the third new fighter to enter service by 1925 was produced in response to an Air Ministry specification, issued in 1922, for a single-seat night fighter. The Hawker Woodcock produced to fill this role used the nine-cylinder Bristol Jupiter radial, and was most remarkable for being the first of a series of fighters from the new Hawker company, set up in 1920 as a successor to the Sopwith firm. Its service was limited to two squadrons, and lasted only until 1928.

The year 1925 also saw the formation of the first five reserve squadrons as advocated by the Salisbury report. Nos 600, 601, 602 and 603 were Auxiliary Air Force units equipped with D.H.9As, while No 502 was a Special Reserve squadron, composed of both regular and reserve officers for twin-engined aircraft, in this case Vimys. The numbers of reserve officers would be increased by the introduction in 1924 of short-service commissions, lasting five years, in order to accelerate the turnover of trained pilots and provide the necessary numbers to bring the reserve squadrons up to full strength in an emergency.

At the same time, however, the brakes were being applied to the expansion scheme which was just getting under way. With the imminent signature of the Treaty of Locarno, by which France, Germany and Belgium agreed to respect the existing national frontiers and Britain and Italy agreed to act as guarantors, and with the prospect of further steps towards disarmament, it was decided at the end of 1925 that completion of the expansion scheme should be deferred to 1935-36.

While the new fighters and reserve squadrons remained in Britain, the units serving overseas were having a busy time. By the summer of 1921 Mustafa Kemal had reorganised the remnants of the Turkish armies, driven the French back into the Lebanon, defeated the Armenians in the east and persuaded the Italians and Russians to leave. When two years of war against the Greeks ended with a Turkish victory in September 1922 the Allied positions east of the Bosphorus Straits were threatened, and while a conference was held in Lausanne to determine a settlement, substantial RAF reinforcements were sent to the area. These comprised a squadron each of Bristol Fighters, Sopwith Snipes and D.H.9As, plus a flight of Nieuport Nightjar naval fighters, from Britain; a squadron of F.2Bs and a flight of Snipes from Egypt; and some of the Fairey IIICs based in Malta. Most of these were based at San Stephano, near the southern end of the Bosphorus Straits, with one F.2B squadron at Kilia, on the Black Sea. Acting as Constantinople Wing, the force remained in Turkey until the conclusion of the Lausanne treaty in July 1923.

Meanwhile, on the borders of the Mosul province in northern Iraq there was considerable unrest among the large Kurdish population, which was agitating for independence, while Britain and Turkey were in dispute over the large oil deposits in the region. RAF operations in connection with these disturbances included the evacuation of local levies from Sulaimanaya in September 1922; the airlift of 480 troops to Kirkuk

The Armstrong Whitworth Siskin Mk IIIA replaced the Mk III's 325-hp Jaguar III engine with a supercharged Jaguar IVS, developing 425 hp to become the standard fighter in the late 1920s

early in 1923, and a similar operation in May 1924; and bombing attacks against a Turkish incursion in September 1924.

By 1925 the RAF strength in Iraq was eight squadrons, including three squadrons of D.H.9As, two of Vernons and one of Snipes at Hinaidi; another D.H.9A squadron at Shaibah; and a squadron of Bristol Fighters at Mosul. Routine tasks included resupply and casualty evacuation, and the patrolling of the large desert areas.

No 14 Squadron in Palestine at this time was equipped with Bristol Fighters and D.H.9As, whose attentions were divided between Ramleh in Palestine and Amman in Transjordan. In Egypt there were a squadron each of D.H.9As, Vimys and F.2Bs at Helwan, Heliopolis and Ismailia respectively, as well as a flying school at Abu Sueir. In India there were a further six squadrons, two of D.H.9As at Risalpur, and single squadrons of F.2Bs at Dardoni, Quetta, Peshawar and Ambala.

A consequence of the wide dispersion of RAF squadrons in disparate parts of the empire was the beginning in 1925 of a series of long-distance flights by aircraft flying in formation to investigate the problems involved and to explore possible air routes for communications. One of the first of these was made by three D.H.9As in October and November, and involved a round trip between Cairo and Kano, Nigeria. Imperial Airways had been incorporated the year before, absorbing the existing independent airlines, and while the question of the best type of aircraft to use for long-distance passenger services – aeroplanes, airships or flying boats – would not be decided for some time, the RAF would have an important role in pioneering the air routes they would use.

Left: A flight of Hawker Woodcocks, third of the new post-war fighters, which served with two squadrons from 1925 to 1928

Below: The Bristol Fighter continued in service as an army co-operation machine throughout the 1920s both at home and overseas

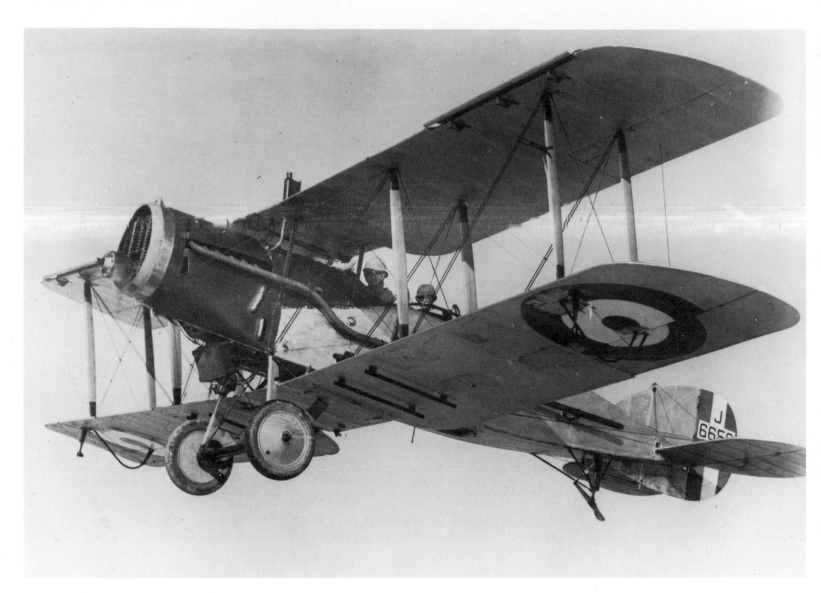

Above: Bristol F.2Bs were the mainstay of the RAF squadrons stationed in India in the 1920s

Right: Airco D.H.10 Amiens and crew at Heliopolis

Above: Loading the desert airmail onto a D.H.9A at Heliopolis

Left: Hawker Harts over the rugged terrain of the North-West Frontier

4 IMPERIAL DEFENCE, 1926-34

During 1926 the Admiralty's last serious challenge to the RAF's independence was defeated. The Colwyn Committee of the previous year, the last of a series established to investigate the question, had concluded that all air work should remain under the control of the Air Ministry, and in 1926 this policy was approved by the prime minister.

For operational purposes the three naval co-operation squadrons formed in 1920 had been reorganised as flights aboard aircraft carriers in 1923, and were under Admiralty control, but the majority of the pilots were RAF officers, and all flying training was carried out by the RAF. As such, the RAF officers at sea served in Coastal Area, one of four Area Commands in Britain, which also included coastal patrol flights, experimental stations and recruiting depots. All other home-based units were organised into Nos 1 and 7 Groups and No 11 Wing, except for the independent Area Commands of Cranwell and Halton.

In 1925, as part of the restructuring necessitated by the implementation of the expansion scheme for home defence, all home defence squadrons became part of a new command, Air Defence of Great Britain. ADGB was, in turn, subdivided into three Area Commands: Wessex Bombing Area comprised all regular bombing squadrons except Nos 15 and 22, which formed part of the Aeroplane and Armament Experimental Establishment at Martlesham Heath and were used for armaments testing; Fighting Area incorporated fighter squadrons and No 24 (Communications) Squadron, which was based near London and provided transport for government and Air Ministry officials and RAF personnel as well as training for RAF officers serving at the Air Ministry; and No 1 Air Defence Group was composed of the new auxiliary bombing squadrons.

As a result of this reorganisation, Coastal Area retained command of the coastal stations, embarked flights and recruiting depots, but the experimental establishments such as A&AEE were transferred to Inland Area. The other components of Inland Area were the army co-operation squadrons and the Schools of Army Co-operation and of Photography, which together formed No 22 Group, while No 23 Group comprised the three Flying Training Schools (Nos 1, 2 and 5), the Central Flying School, where flying instructors were trained, and the specialist schools of Armament and Gunnery, Technical Training and Electrical and Wireless.

Overseas commands remained unchanged. Middle East Command was responsible for units in Egypt, Palestine, Transjordan and Aden; Mediterranean Command had its headquarters on Malta; and Iraq and India each had their own commands. The theoretical requirements of home defence contrasted with the practical demands on the overseas squadrons, so there were continuing investigations of the possi-

Previous page: A Short Singapore Mk III about to become airborne

bilities for rapid reinforcement of the latter.

The Cairo-Kano flight of 1925 was followed in the spring of 1926 by a more ambitious flight from Cairo to South Africa and back. The aircraft used for this expedition were four Fairey IIIDs, descendants of the wartime Fairey IIIs which saw extensive service with the Fleet Air Arm during the 1920s as well as equipping No 202 Squadron in Malta. The type could use either wheels or floats, and for the 14,000-mile round trip between Cairo and the Cape they were fitted with wheels, before transferring to floats on their return to Cairo to continue the journey to England. The following year the first IIIFs entered RAF service, eventually serving with six squadrons in Aden, Palestine, Egypt, the Sudan and Malta as well as at home.

The main attribute of the Fairey III series was their versatility, but for long-distance cruises involving extended sea crossings flying boats were regarded as safer, as well as having more scope for enlargement than float planes. Among the RAF's first twin-engined flying boats was the Supermarine Southampton, early examples of which had wooden hulls. Two Southamptons made a 7000-mile (11,270-km) cruise from Felixstowe to Cairo and back in 1926, and the following year four flying boats of different types made a Baltic cruise, visiting Scandinavian capitals.

As well as a Southampton I, the flying boats that travelled to the Baltic in August 1926 comprised

another twin-engined type, the all-metal Short Singapore, and two triple-engined boats, the Saunders-Roe Valkyrie and Blackburn Iris II; the former was built of wood while the latter was a metal-hulled rebuild of the original Iris I. The results of this test cruise indicated that metal hulls had definite advantages, and eventually both the Iris and the Singapore, as well as metal-hulled Southamptons, were produced for the RAF.

Only five Irises were built, though rebuilding and re-engining resulted in as many different models, while four Iris VIs were renamed Perth on entering service in 1934. Only one squadron, No 209, was ever equipped with Irises and Perths. The Iris was the biggest RAF aircraft of its day, and the Perth, which was equipped to carry a 37-mm COW gun in the bow, was the RAF's biggest biplane flying boat.

Meanwhile, the introduction of the light alloy hull on the Southampton II was followed by one of the most ambitious of all the long-distance flights of the period. On 17 October 1927 the Far East Flight of four Southampton IIs left Plymouth on a cruise that would ultimately cover some 27,000 miles (43,470 km) and last over a year. Travelling through the Mediterranean, down the Persian Gulf and round the coast of India, the Far East Flight reached Singapore at the beginning of March 1928, and in May the cruise was resumed, taking in a circumnavigation of Australia

The Short Singapore Mk I was developed into the four-engined Mk III, which equipped six squadrons during the 1930s

and visits to Japan, Hong Kong and Burma before returning to Singapore. There the flight became No 205 Squadron, the first Far Eastern squadron of the RAF, before carrying out further survey flights.

As well as No 205 Squadron, Southamptons formed a further four squadrons, three at home and one based at Basra in Iraq. The Iraq squadron, No 203, replaced its Southamptons with the Rangoon development of the civil Short Calcutta in 1931, but the others remained in service until the mid-1930s. The Singapore had a more protracted development before the first squadron, No 209, was equipped with Mk IIs in 1932 as replacements for its missing Irises. The Singapore II and its successor, the Mk III, had four engines mounted in tandem pairs, and the latter was the main production version, equipping a total of six squadrons, including two in the Middle East and three at home, as well as No 205 in Singapore, during the later 1930s.

The significance of the RAF's long-distance flights, as distinct from the record-breaking efforts of many private fliers of the time, was that they were conducted by formations of aircraft in carefully planned stages, thus paving the way both for airline services and for the RAF's own routes to the Middle and Far East. Flying boats were particularly useful in this role, as they were able to alight on any reasonably sheltered stretch of water, dispensing with the need for prepared airfields.

Otherwise, operations in the Middle East continued during the second half of the 1920s along the pattern established in Iraq. The standard method of dealing with disturbances relied rather on intimidation than on wholesale destruction. Normally, warnings would be issued, often in the form of leaflets dropped from the air; should further action be required, demonstration bombing raids might be carried out, possibly involving the destruction of buildings, but more often aimed at crops or livestock, and this was avoided where possible. Similar policies were followed on the North-West Frontier of India, though in Palestine, where there was continual conflict between the Arab population and the growing number of Jewish immigrants, air policing was virtually useless for dealing with urban riots.

In addition, during 1927 No 2 Squadron was despatched to Shanghai, where it operated Bristol Fighters from the local racecourse in support of the Shanghai Defence Force for three months. The same year saw No 8 Squadron's D.H.9As posted to Aden, when the RAF was given responsibility for the protectorate, and No 47, also with D.H.9As, stationed in Khartoum. Both squadrons were soon equipped with Fairey IIIFs, some of which were used with floats by No 47 for operations along the Nile.

Another type of operation made possible by the RAF presence in these areas was the rapid deployment of troops to trouble spots. The relatively small troop carriers of the time could not transport large forces, but often the timely appearance of a small number of troops was all that was required. Operating in the opposite direction, aircraft could also be used to

Inset: The Supermarine Scapa was a development of the Southampton, with enclosed flight deck and Rolls-Royce Kestrel engines in place of the Southampton's Napier Lions

Left: One of the six Short Rangoons developed from the Calcutta passenger flying boat for service in Iraq between 1931 and 1935

evacuate vulnerable personnel when a situation could not be controlled, and towards the end of 1928 such a situation was developing in Afghanistan.

King Amanullah had undertaken an extensive tour of the Middle East and Europe during 1928, and was particularly impressed by the reforms which Mustafa Kemal and Shah Reza had introduced in Turkey and Iran. On his return he instituted similar reforms in Afghanistan, but his attempts at secularisation and westernisation were not backed by the resources necessary for their enforcement, and the Shinwari tribe, who had never really been subject to his authority, began a rebellion. By the middle of December the situation had become so serious that the British Minister in Kabul, Sir Francis Humphrys, asked for an evacuation of the staff of the legation.

Since the only transport aircraft in India at the time were D.H.9As and Wapitis, a Victoria was despatched from Iraq, followed a few days later by two more. The evacuation began on 23 December, and with the aid of another five Victorias which arrived by the middle of February 1929 a total of 586 men, women and children left the country, including Amanullah himself along with his family, the entire staff of the legation and a number of other foreigners.

The Kabul operation, involving as it did not only the transfer of the troop carriers from Hinaidi to Risalpur – a distance of some 2800 miles (4508 km) – and the successful completion of many thousands of miles of flying on a total of 84 sorties through extremely hazardous mountains, but also the transfer of No 216 Squadron's Victorias from Heliopolis to Hinaidi as replacements for those of No 70, was greeted as a triumph for the RAF. It was certainly a fitting climax to the 10 post-war years that had begun with another flight to India and another mission to Kabul: at the same time, it marked the beginning of Trenchard's last year as Chief of the Air Staff, although by no means the end of his influence on the air force.

Before his retirement at the end of 1929 Trenchard was responsible for two documents which were to establish RAF policy for another decade and more. The first of these, entitled *The War Object of an Air Force*, was produced in May 1928 in response to a request from the Commandant of the Imperial Defence College, who felt that the manuals of all three services should embody a common definition of the principles of warfare. Outlining his views on the role of air power in pursuit of the overall aim of 'defeating the enemy nation', Trenchard accepted the stated objectives of navy and army – namely to destroy or neutralise the opposing navy, and to destroy the enemy's main forces on the battlefield – and added his own definition of the object of the air force: 'To break down the enemy's means of resistance by attacks on objectives selected as most likely to achieve that end.'

There was little anyone could object to in such a broad definition, but in Trenchard's selection of those objectives there were problems. Dismissing the idea that the air force should be directed against the

A flight of Fairey IIIFs on the
River Nile at Khartoum in the
Sudan during their survey flight in
1934

enemy's armed forces on the grounds that this was both difficult and unnecessary, he concluded that the advantage of air power was its ability to 'pass over' armies and navies and 'attack the centres of production, transportation and communication from which the enemy war effort is maintained'. Such targets, he went on, would include munitions factories producing munitions and any other military supplies 'from boots to battleships', as well as docks, railway workshops and all forms of communications. Disclaiming the idea that such attacks were either illegal or immoral on the grounds that all the targets he mentioned were legitimate military targets, he further emphasised his view that such a form of warfare was not only legitimate and effective but also inevitable, and would certainly be practised by an enemy. Anticipating the objection that such strategic attacks had achieved very little in the previous European war, he pointed out that these had been carried out on a very limited scale by an inadequate force, but had nevertheless caused serious interruption to war production.

The fundamental errors in this view of aerial warfare have been demonstrated on many occasions. In the first place, Trenchard overestimated the damage his bombers could cause to the centres of production he felt it necessary to attack, partly through underestimating the degree of opposition they would encounter; and in the second he overestimated the effect on the morale of the civilian population of bombing attacks. It may be easy to see this with the benefit of hindsight, and certainly Trenchard could not have foreseen the development of radar and the immense advantage this would give to anti-aircraft defences.

But he had himself written that his own Independent Force day bombers in 1918 had had to fight 'practically from the front line to their objective, and from there home again'. Furthermore he knew that bombing accuracy was seriously degraded in night attacks and had dismissed the idea of producing long-range fighters as bomber escorts on the grounds that more fighters could only be produced at the expense of bomber production. In fact, his basic idea was that the nation that could stand being bombed the longest would win in the end.

Trenchard's final contribution to air policy before his departure came in November 1929 in the form of a paper entitled *The Fuller Employment of Air Power in Imperial Defence*. In this document, prepared for the Air Minister, Trenchard pointed out the relative uselessness of anything but an armed police force in the urban strife suffered in Palestine, but contrasted this with the success of air control in the sparsely populated expanses of Transjordan. On this basis, he recommended a systematic extension of air control to cover not only the North-West Frontier, the Sudan and British East and West Africa, but also the use of flying boats to replace naval patrols in the Red Sea and

Persian Gulf, and the introduction of bombers for coastal defence in place of the traditional, and generally obsolete, batteries of coast defence guns.

Trenchard's successor as Chief of the Air Staff was Air Chief Marshal Sir John Salmond, who since his appointment as AOC Iraq had commanded the Air Defence of Great Britain and been Air Member for Personnel. In 1933 he was succeeded by his elder brother Sir Geoffrey, who was a former AOC India, in which capacity he had organised the evacuation of Kabul, and more recently had been in command of ADGB. In the event, the latter became ill and died before he could take up the post, and on 22 May Air Chief Marshal Sir Edward Ellington replaced him.

The intervening years saw little progress made towards the old target of 52 home defence squadrons, let alone the implementation of Trenchard's schemes. Economic depression and the approaching Disarmament Conference in Geneva combined to inhibit further expenditure on the armed forces, and the 1930 Air Estimates postponed the date for the completion of the 1923 expansion programme to 1938.

In fact, the early years of the new decade brought British proposals for a reduction in the strength of air forces generally and the outlawing of aerial bombing. This doctrine was spelled out in a White Paper of November 1932, at the same time as the British proposals were presented at Geneva. The detailed

This Iris V, one of three converted from Mk IIIs, was destroyed by a gale the day after this photograph was taken in January 1933

A Hawker Hind, one of the many derivatives of the Hart, distinguished by a supercharged engine and cut-down rear cockpit

Above right: The Hawker Hardy general purpose version of the Hart was produced for service in the Middle East

Right: The RAF's last all-wood fighter, the Gloster Gamecock development of the Grebe, served with four squadrons in the late 1920s and inherited its predecessor's reputation as an aerobatic aircraft

recommendations included a reduction of the air forces of the 'leading Powers' (that is, Britain, France, Italy, Japan, the Soviet Union and the United States) to the same level as Britain's, to be followed by an all-round one-third reduction, a limit on the maximum weight of military aircraft and the internationalisation of civil aviation.

The response to this plan was less than overwhelming: Japanese forces were already bombing China, and Germany had little interest in proposals which assumed there should be no German air force at all. Another year brought new British proposals for a limitation on air forces to 500 aircraft, but within months Germany had resigned from the conference for good, and by the beginning of 1934 there was a change of policy. The Air Estimates for that year were increased slightly to allow for an additional four RAF squadrons, two of which were to be retained for home defence. At the same time, the German defence budget was increased massively, whereupon the French formally rejected the air disarmament scheme.

By this stage Germany, rather than France, had been recognised as the 'ultimate potential enemy', and by July a new scheme for air force expansion had been approved by the Cabinet. Known as Scheme A, the new plan envisaged the creation of 33 new squadrons for home defence in addition to the 42 then in existence, plus another eight for service with the Fleet Air Arm and overseas. Specifically, these were to include 41 squadrons of bombers, 28 of fighters, two of torpedo bombers and four of reconnaissance aircraft (in place of, respectively, 28, 13 and none) in addition to the existing four flying boat and five army co-operation squadrons. The date set for completion of the scheme was March 1939.

The modest expansion that had taken place in the 10 years preceding the announcement of this plan had

involved an equally modest improvement in the capabilities of the aircraft provided. The Armstrong Whitworth Siskin III that had entered service with two fighter squadrons in 1924 was improved in its Mk IIIA version by the use of a supercharged 425-hp Jaguar IVS engine. The use of supercharging enhanced performance at altitude and allowed the service ceiling to be raised to 27,000 ft (8230 m), with the result that the Siskin IIIA became the standard RAF fighter of the late 1920s, entering service with No 111 Squadron in September 1926 and eventually equipping a total of 11 fighter squadrons.

A contemporary of the Siskin IIIA, the Gloster Gamecock, was developed from the same company's Grebe by the substitution of the 425-hp Bristol Jupiter VI engine for the earlier type's Jaguar, and between 1925 and 1928 five fighter squadrons were equipped with Gamecocks, two of them as night fighter units. However, the Gamecock's career was curtailed by a large number of crashes, and during 1928 three of the squadrons using it switched to Siskins, which also replaced Grebes.

Another innovation in terms of powerplant was introduced by the Fairey Fox. The prototype of this outstanding light bomber was built in 1925 using the Curtiss D-12 engine, streamlined cowling, wing-skin radiators and metal propeller that had helped the Curtiss R2C racer win the Schneider Trophy for America in 1923. The resulting increase of more than 40 mph (64 km/h) over the earlier Fairey Fawn so impressed Trenchard that on his own initiative he ordered a squadron's worth of the new bomber. These were powered by the Fairey Felix, a licence-built version of the D-12, and with a top speed of 156 mph (251 km/h), were as fast as the Siskin fighters. The Fox entered service with No 12 Squadron in June 1926, which remained the only unit to use the type.

The Hawker Horsley III torpedo bomber development of the basic Horsley bomber served with No 36 Squadron in Singapore from 1930 to 1935

Inset: The Armstrong Whitworth Siskin IIIA with supercharged Jaguar IVS engine served with 11 squadrons in the late 1920s until replaced by the Fury and Bulldog

An Armstrong Whitworth Atlas demonstrates the use of its pick-up hook, standard equipment for army co-operation aircraft of this period

The same year saw the introduction of another new bomber to replace the disappointing Fawn. This was the Hawker Horsley, produced to meet an official specification of 1923 for a Rolls-Royce Condor-powered long-range day bomber. The all-wood Horsley that resulted could carry up to 1600 lb (726 kg) of bombs or a 2150-lb (975-kg) torpedo in its later versions, last of which was the all-metal Mk III, developed as a specialised torpedo carrier and taken to Singapore by No 36 Squadron in 1930. Another three squadrons used Horsleys at home between 1926 and 1933.

Meanwhile, in 1924 a specification was issued for a replacement for the Bristol Fighter as an army co-operation aircraft. The successful prototype was produced by Armstrong Whitworth in the form of the Atlas, a fabric-covered metal biplane powered by a 450-hp Jaguar IVC engine and designed to carry out the various functions of ground attack, message pick-up (by means of a hook below the fuselage) and photographic reconnaissance. Four 20-lb (9-kg) bombs could be carried and armament was the standard forward-firing Vickers and Scarff-mounted Lewis used on virtually all two-seaters of the time. Five squadrons at home and one in Egypt were equipped with the Atlas between 1927 and 1931, while another 146 were built as trainers; the last were retired from squadron service in 1934.

By 1927 it was becoming necessary to look for a replacement for the general-purpose D.H.9A, and a specification issued that year called for such a type with better performance and able to lift a heavier load, while using as many D.H.9A components as possible in the interests of economy. A general-purpose version of the Atlas was prepared to meet this requirement, but the successful design was that of the Wapiti, produced by Westland, who had been responsible for developing the D.H.9A. The principal production version of the Wapiti was the Mk IIA, which was equipped to use wheel, float or ski undercarriage. Eight squadrons in India used Wapitis during the 1930s, two of which were still equipped with the type in 1940, and the three D.H.9A squadrons in Iraq also received Wapitis as replacements.

In contrast to the general trend towards multirole aircraft, the Boulton and Paul Sidestrand, which entered service with No 101 Squadron in 1929, was a specialised bomber powered by twin Jupiter engines and characterised by a distinctively curved fuselage profile. Performance was good, with a top speed of 140 mph (225 km/h), and bombing accuracy was exceptional. Lewis guns were provided for the bomb-aimer in the nose, and in dorsal and ventral positions, so that the Sidestrand represented one of the few RAF bombers of the time that could have carried out the kind of attack Trenchard had advocated, but one squadron was all that could be afforded.

A contemporary of the Sidestrand produced in slightly greater quantity was the Handley Page Hinaidi, an all-metal development of the Hyderabad

The Hawker Hart served in large numbers during the 1930s in its basic role of light bomber, as well as forming the basis for numerous derivatives

powered by two Jupiter air-cooled radials in place of the earlier type's water-cooled Lions. After the prototype had participated in the Kabul airlift, two RAF squadrons were equipped with Hinaidis, and a troop-carrying version, named the Clive, was used by the RAF's Heavy Transport Flight at Lahore.

Meanwhile, a 1926 specification for a high-performance day bomber had resulted in one of the outstanding designs of the decade in the form of the Hawker Hart. With a top speed of 184 mph (296 km/h) the Hart was, like the earlier Fox, a serious challenge to contemporary fighters and it became the RAF's standard day bomber until 1937, serving with seven squadrons at home from 1930 and with another two in India, as well as with most of the auxiliary air force squadrons.

In fact, the Hart proved so impressive that a special version designated the Hart Fighter was produced with a supercharged version of the Rolls-Royce Kestrel engine and twin Vickers guns in the nose. After trials with a flight of No 23 Squadron from 1931, the Demon was ordered as a production two-seat fighter, and ultimately equipped six fighter squadrons in the mid-1930s as well as serving briefly with flights of another three. The ultimate development of the Demon involved the provision of a partially screened, hydraulically operated turret for the Lewis gun in the rear cockpit, in order to enable the weapon to be aimed against the slipstream.

Other fighters which had appeared in the meantime were the Bristol Bulldog and Hawker Fury, which first entered service in 1929 and 1931 respectively. The

Bulldog was produced in response to an official requirement for a Siskin replacement. Powered by a Jupiter engine, the Bulldog became the principal fighter of the early 1930s, equipping 10 of the home-based fighter squadrons. The later Fury used an in-line Rolls-Royce Kestrel in contrast to the Bulldog's air-cooled radial engine, and was the first RAF fighter capable of exceeding 200 mph (322 km/h), though only three squadrons were equipped with the original Mk I production version. This was a result of financial rather than military considerations: in its prototype form as the Hawker Hornet it had proved the only fighter capable of catching the same company's Hart bomber when first flown in 1929.

The same financial stringency that limited production of the Fury I was responsible for the continuing emphasis on multirole aircraft, the next example of which was the Fairey Gordon. The Gordon was derived from the Fairey IIIF, replacing its predecessor's water-cooled Lion with an air-cooled Armstrong Siddeley Panther and taking over from it with the four IIIF squadrons in the Middle East and East Africa, replacing Bristol Fighters with a fifth and serving with two further home-based squadrons.

Another development in the field of general purpose types was the conversion of the Westland Wapiti to produce the Wallace. These were used by four of the Special Reserve Squadrons in the mid-1930s, and the Mk II version featured a glazed canopy over the two cockpits.

The early 1930s also saw the advent of a specialised torpedo bomber in the shape of the Vickers Vildebeest. Among the five squadrons to use Vildebeests were Nos 36 and 100 in Singapore: these were still in service at the time of the Japanese invasion in 1941, and the last Vildebeest squadron was formed as late as 1939 in Ceylon.

The last new aircraft to enter service before the expansion scheme got under way was a new night bomber from Handley Page, the Heyford. Innovations introduced by the Heyford included the attachment of the fuselage to the upper, rather than the lower, wing, and the installation of a retractable ventral turret. Fortunately for the RAF, this was the last biplane heavy bomber, and none of the total of 11 squadrons which used the type between its introduction in 1933 and its retirement in 1939 was still flying the type at the outbreak of war.

The Vickers Vildebeest torpedo bomber replaced the Horsley, and still equipped two squadrons in Singapore at the time of the Japanese invasion

The Bristol Bulldog was the principal replacement for the Siskin, serving with 10 squadrons between 1929 and 1936 and forming the bulk of the fighter defence force during the early 1930s

73

Despite the financial constraints on aircraft development and procurement during these years, the RAF had managed some pure record-breaking and racing activity. The first of a series of attempts on the endurance record was made in May 1927, when Flight Lieutenants C R Carr and L E M Gillman took off from Cranwell in a Hawker Horsley carrying 1100 gallons of fuel compared with a normal capacity for the type of 230 gallons (1046 l). The planned destination was India, but the flight ended 3420 miles (5500 km) away when the engine cut out and the aircraft was ditched in the Persian Gulf. This would have beaten the previous record, but for the fact that Charles Lindbergh had chosen the same day for his record-breaking flight from New York to Paris.

A fresh attempt was made in April 1929, using a specially built Fairey monoplane: this time the flight covered 4130 miles (6649 km) before being forced to land at Karachi because of unfavourable headwinds. Tragedy marred the next attempt in the same aircraft, which ended with a crash on a hillside near Tunis. However, a new Fairey monoplane was built, and in February 1933 Squadron Leader O R Gayford and Flight Lieutenant G E Nicholetts flew this aircraft 5341 miles (8599 km) from Cranwell to Walvis Bay in South Africa, taking just under $57\frac{1}{2}$ hours and finally claiming the record for Britain.

The pursuit of speed was also rewarded with success. Successive developments of the Supermarine racer designated S.5, S.6 and S.6B won the Schneider Trophy in successive contests held in 1927, 1929 and 1931, though the last event had only the British entry, to claim the trophy outright for Britain. And to crown this success the S.6B established a new world speed record of 407.5 mph (656 km/h) on 29 September 1931, 16 days after the third Schneider success.

Throughout the inter-war years, too, the annual RAF displays at the old Hendon aerodrome, requisitioned during the First World War and retained afterwards by the Air Ministry, became favourite events with the public, attracting hundreds of thousands of spectators. Exhibitions of new aeroplanes, displays of aerobatics and demonstrations of formation flying combined to form a brilliant spectacle.

The pattern was established by the RAF Tournament of July 1920, when 40,000 people saw mock dogfights, a formation of Bristol Fighters performing to radio commands, parachute descents from a V/1500 and aerobatics by a Sopwith Camel. Billed as the RAF Pageant, the 1921 performances included mock attacks on bombers and a kite balloon and the destruction of a model village, while in 1922 a static display was added, including such new types as an Avro Aldershot. The following year the new types on display included the Gloster Grebe, which was also given an aerial demonstration, and the set piece featured Vickers Vernons landing troops to relieve a besieged garrison.

The Supermarine S.5 which won the 1927 Schneider Trophy race at an average speed of 281.66 mph (453.3 km/h)

In 1925 the rain that had marred earlier events was replaced by perfect weather for 80,000 spectators, who saw a succession of new prototypes along with aerobatics from the fighters and formation flying by two whole squadrons of D.H.9As. The spectacular finale featured a mock naval battle in which a British cargo vessel was attacked by an enemy armed merchant cruiser, before a Seagull appeared on the scene to summon help in the form of a flight of Flycatchers and five Blackburn Darts, which dropped their dummy torpedoes to demolish the hostile vessel.

Official secrecy kept many new prototypes out of the displays, but as the years passed the evolution of the RAF's aircraft was clearly reflected. Parachute descents became standard features, and in 1926 there were some real novelties: an Avro autogyro and a tailless Westland Pterodactyl, as well as the Fairey Fox with its Curtiss engine. The Boulton and Paul Sidestrand, Fairey IIIF, Westland Wapiti and Bristol Bulldog were among the new types in 1927, when operations in Iraq were reflected in the simulated rescue of a desert garrison while Fairey Foxes bombed and machine gunned their attackers; and the Middle East again provided the theme for the centrepiece in 1928, with the simulated destruction of an oil refinery.

The displays continued during the next decade. In June 1930 the exhibits included the Supermarine S.6 and Gloster VI Schneider Trophy seaplanes alongside the more familiar types, with only a D.H.77 low-wing monoplane giving a hint of things to come: the airship *R.101* put in an appearance, leaking steadily and with only three engines running, while an aero-

batic innovation was provided by three Siskins which performed tied together by flag-hung rubber cords. Barely three months later the airship had been lost in a crash.

In 1931 there were the usual spectacles, but also some more practical innovations: a Vickers Virginia was refuelled in the air, and a new compressed-air catapult for launching aircraft from ships was demonstrated. The following years saw processions of new flying boats and varied collections of prototypes, and by 1934 some significant new ones: the Boulton Paul Overstrand with its powered nose turret, and the Supermarine Type 224, a low-wing monoplane, still with fixed undercarriage but carrying four machine guns and bearing the unofficial name Spitfire.

The Display continued as an annual event until 1937, but the night following the 1934 event, 30 June, was Germany's 'Night of the Long Knives', when dozens of Hitler's former SA supporters were murdered, and gloomier prospects for international peace were reflected in a more business-like look to the warplanes. By 1936 biplanes were absent from the exhibition of new types, which included Spitfire, Hurricane, Battle and Wellington prototypes: instead, the biplanes appeared in the form of historic aircraft, with a replica of the Wright Flyer joining Camel, S.E.5a and Bristol Fighter.

The culmination of the series of displays came in 1937, and again there was a demonstration of First World War types, but this time the highlight was the massed flypast by no fewer than 260 bombers – Whitleys, Wellesleys, Blenheims, Hinds and Vildebeests – in five columns, watched by 200,000 spectators.

One of the two Supermarine S.6Bs developed for the 1931 Schneider Trophy race, won by S1596 at an average speed of just over 340 mph (547 km/h)

Right: Aerial view of the scene at an RAF display at Hendon in the early 1920s

Far right: Aircraft on the ground and in the air at Hendon in 1922

Far right: Hawker Furys preparing for take-off at the 1937 Hendon display

Right: The scene at Hendon in 1937, with the set for the finale in the background

5 REARMING FOR WAR 1935-39

The Royal Air Force celebrated the silver jubilee of King George V in July 1935 by staging the biggest flypast that had ever been seen. In the morning of 6 July the king visited RAF Mildenhall where a total of 356 aircraft and their crews, representing 25 regular and 12 auxiliary squadrons as well as coast defence units, formed a static display. In the afternoon he was driven to RAF Duxford, where he watched as 20 of the squadrons from Mildenhall flew overhead.

However, the aircraft themselves were ominously old-fashioned. Two squadrons of Heyfords, five of Harts, two of Audaxes, one of Demons, six of Bulldogs and three of Furys, representing the heavy and light bomber, army co-operation and fighter strength of the force, were followed by No 19 Squadron with the newest fighter, the Gloster Gauntlet. The Heyfords maintained the stately pace of 98 mph (158 km/h), while the fighters were hardly more exciting at 120 mph (193 km/h).

The Gauntlet had entered service with No 19 Squadron only two months before the flypast, yet it was derived from the Gloster SS.18 which had flown for the first time as long ago as January 1929. The SS.18 had actually been a contender for the fighter contract that went instead to the Bristol Bulldog, but now the Gauntlet was in production as a Bulldog

replacement, and within two years 14 squadrons would be equipped with the type: expansion was under way, but for the time being it would be based on clearly obsolescent aircraft.

At the beginning of 1935 the first examples of the Vickers Vincent, a general purpose derivative of the Vildebeest, had entered service as a replacement for the Fairey IIIFs and Westland Wapitis with the overseas squadrons. Slightly better performance was offered by another new general purpose type, the Hawker Hardy version of the Hart bomber. The first of the 47 built went to No 30 Squadron in Iraq in April, and were later passed on to two other squadrons in the Middle East and East Africa. In September and November the two bomber transport squadrons in the Middle East received Valentias, essentially Victoria Mk VIs under another name, and most of which were simply Victorias fitted with slightly more powerful models of the Pegasus engine.

The only new aircraft to show any real innovation was the Boulton Paul Overstrand, a stronger, more powerful and more comfortable development of the company's earlier Sidestrand. The main interest in the Overstrand, however, was its pneumatically operated nose turret, which balanced the weight of the gunner on his seat against the weight of the installation to give automatic traverse and elevation as the gunner

Previous page: Supermarine Spitfire Is

Bristol Bulldogs of No 17 Squadron. The Bulldog was still one of the principal RAF fighters in 1935

adjusted his aim. No 101 Squadron was the only unit to operate the Overstrand, which was still fitted with a fixed undercarriage, and the single Lewis gun mounted in the turret seemed hardly worth such an elaborate mounting.

Nevertheless, in the absence of anything better, it was decided that new squadrons should continue to be formed with light bombers, so that at least there would be trained crews for the new, advanced types that were currently being ordered off the drawing board in an attempt to cut out the lengthy development process.

Accordingly, the next new type to appear was the Hawker Hind, which began to enter service in the following January. Yet another Hart derivative, the Hind embodied few major changes apart from the use of a fully supercharged Kestrel V engine and a cut-down rear cockpit to improve the gunner's field of fire. The new model superseded the Hart in six home-based day bomber squadrons, but more important were the 25 new squadrons that were formed with Hinds between 1936 and 1938, while altogether 14 auxiliary squadrons used the type. By 1939 all the new squadrons had converted to new monoplane bombers.

In the meantime, expansion scheme A had been superseded by the much more ambitious scheme F, approved by the Cabinet in February 1936. The increased urgency that had provoked this and a series of earlier new schemes derived from the realisation in the spring of 1935 that the new German air force, the Luftwaffe, was already bigger than the RAF. The overall aim of scheme F was an air force of 161 squadrons, 124 of them based in Britain, by March 1939. The home force was to consist of 68 squadrons of bombers, 30 of fighters, two of torpedo bombers, seven land-based and six flying-boat reconnaissance squadrons and 11 for army co-operation.

The new scheme restored the emphasis on bombers, which was Trenchard's legacy. Not the least of its requirements was an increase in the total number of home-based aircraft from 547 to 1736. Overseas strength was to enjoy a less dramatic but still substantial increase from 24 to 37 squadrons, representing 468 aircraft instead of the 265 in March 1934. Moreover, the single-engined day bombers were to be replaced by the new medium bombers, which would equip a total of 48 squadrons, and adequate war reserves were to be provided by raising the initial establishment of 29 of them from 12 aircraft to 18. The underlying intention was to build an air force strong enough to deter any German attack through the Low Countries and Belgium.

As it happened, while this new scheme was being worked out a major overseas deployment was under way. Following the Italian invasion of Ethiopia in October 1935 several squadrons were shipped to the Middle East while some of those already in the area were moved nearer to the war zone, though there was no direct intervention in the conflict. A squadron of IIIFs moved from Egypt to the Sudan, where it was joined by two squadrons of Gordons from Britain, and another squadron of Gordons was formed in Kenya. A squadron each of Demons and Harts were shipped to Aden, two similar units going as reinforcements to Egypt, where a third Demon squadron was formed, and a squadron of Vildebeest torpedo bombers and another new Demon squadron were based on Malta. Flying boats were also deployed, with the Singapore squadron from Iraq moving to Aden, Rangoons and Stranraers – the latter being improved Southamptons – stationed in Gibraltar, and a squadron of Supermarine Scapas, also derived from the Southampton, with another of Singapores based in Egypt. All these remained at their new bases until October 1936, some months after the Italian invasion had been completed.

By this time the first really modern aircraft were in service, in the form of the Avro Anson. This was based on a commercial airliner, and became the RAF's first monoplane with a retractable undercarriage when the first examples joined No 48 Squadron for air-crew training in March 1936. Both the undercarriage and the dorsal turret were manually operated, but the Anson gave excellent service as a trainer – during 1936 No 48 had no less than 80 on strength at the School of Air Navigation at Manston – as well as serving with coastal reconnaissance squadrons.

Three months later the old ADGB Command was replaced by four new commands. Bomber, Fighter, Coastal and Training Commands, each with its own headquarters, were constituted with respective strengths of six, three, three and four groups. At the same time, in order to meet the demand for new aircraft and engines the government financed a system of 'shadow' factories which were operated by various motor car manufacturers. Initially, five companies were involved in the production of the Bristol Pegasus and Mercury engines that were in greatest demand, some in the production of components which the others assembled.

Among the first to benefit from the new supply of engines was the Handley Page Harrow, which was also one of the first of the new bombers ordered at the design stage without waiting for a prototype. Five squadrons were equipped with Harrows during 1937, and the type was notable for its use of powered turrets in both nose and tail positions. These turrets still

Previous page: King George V and party with Rolls-Royces in front of a Handley Page Heyford at RAF Mildenhall, Suffolk, during the Jubilee Review, 6 July 1935

The Bristol Blenheim I was one of the most advanced types in service when it joined No 114 Squadron in March 1937

mounted only a single Lewis gun, but they embodied a driving mechanism produced by Nash and Thompson, whose turrets were to become standard equipment on the RAF's heavy bombers.

The Harrow was also a monoplane, though not the first monoplane heavy bomber: the previous November No 38 Squadron had received the Fairey Hendon, six years after the prototype had flown for the first time. Only 14 Hendons were built, and No 38 was the only squadron to be fully equipped with the type, though one flight was detached to reform No 115 Squadron in June 1937.

November 1936 also saw the appearance in service of the Fury II, with a more powerful 640-hp Kestrel VI engine and fairings on the undercarriage wheels. The Fury II was produced as a replacement for the Fury Is while a more extensively revised version using the ultimately unsuccessful steam-cooled Goshawk engine was under development. The latter had been developed to meet a 1930 specification for a new fighter having

a top speed of at least 250 mph (403 km/h), carrying four Vickers guns and with improved performance all round. The further specification of the Goshawk engine meant that none of the aircraft originally designed to meet this requirement was acceptable, and in the end the Mercury-engined Gloster Gladiator, a development of the Gauntlet, was ordered instead.

The first Gladiators joined a flight of No 1 Squadron to form No 72 Squadron in February 1937, and the RAF's last biplane fighter was significant in its doubling of the previously accepted armament of two Vickers machine guns. Two of these were in the nose and one in each lower wing, and the Vickers guns were subsequently replaced by .303-in Brownings, with the considerably higher rate of fire of 1200 rds/min. The Gladiator had an enclosed cockpit, but was otherwise outmoded for a fighter of the late 1930s, having a fixed-pitch wooden airscrew and offering no armour protection for the pilot. Nevertheless, eight fighter squadrons were equipped with Gladiators during

1937, and while these were soon superseded by Hurricanes and Spitfires, the type saw service subsequently in the Middle East, usually only briefly as equipment for newly formed squadrons.

The spring of 1937 also saw the arrival of several of the new bombers produced under the expansion scheme, with Whitleys, Blenheims, Battles and Wellesleys all entering service in March and April. The Armstrong Whitworth Whitley had been designed to meet the same specification as the Harrow, and was at first armed with single Vickers guns in manually operated nose and tail turrets. However, the Mk III version introduced a powered turret for the nose guns, with an additional retractable ventral turret mounting two Brownings, and the Mk IV dispensed with the ventral installation in favour of a four-gun Nash and Thompson tail turret. The main production version, the Mk V of 1939, extended the tail slightly to give the rear gunner a better field of fire.

The Bristol Blenheim, by contrast, was armed with the traditional single forward-firing Vickers, though this was mounted in the port wing and was soon replaced by a Browning, and a Lewis gun for rearward defence. A retractable turret had replaced the old Scarff ring as a mounting, and the gun itself was replaced by the Vickers gas-operated, as opposed to recoil-operated, K gun. The Blenheim's main form of defence was, however, its speed, which at 285 mph (459 km/h) allowed it to outpace most contemporary fighters with ease. This, in turn, was a result of its truly modern design, incorporating such features as stressed skin construction, retractable undercarriage and variable-pitch propellers. On the other hand, only 1000 lb (454 kg) of bombs could be carried, and the type was to remain in production long after it had become obsolescent.

The other two new bombers were both single-engined, the last such aircraft to be built for the RAF. The Fairey Battle was produced to meet a 1932 specification for a day bomber able to carry 1000 lb (454 kg) of bombs 1000 miles (1609 km) at 200 mph (322 km/h). Although these figures represented considerable improvements over those of the Harts and Hinds the new bomber was intended to replace, neither the Battle's maximum speed of 241 mph (388 km/h) nor its armament of single wing-mounted Browning and manually aimed Vickers K gun would offer much protection against the new fighters it was to meet in combat a few years later.

The Vickers Wellesley was the first RAF aircraft to use the geodetic form of construction originally developed by Barnes Wallis for the airship *R.100*. Composed of small sections of rolled or pressed light alloy riveted together in basket-work fashion, the geodetic method had the dual advantages of reduced weight and ease of repair, though it precluded an internal bomb bay and the Wellesley's bombs were carried in nacelles under the wings. As well as serving

with six Bomber Command squadrons, the Wellesley was used by the Long-Range Development Flight to establish a new distance record of 7162 miles (11,526 km) in November 1938, when two examples completed a flight from Ismailia in Egypt to Darwin in northern Australia.

An indication of the sort of opposition the new bombers would have to face came towards the end of 1937 with the introduction of the Hawker Hurricane. The RAF's first fighter capable of exceeding 300 mph (483 km/h) in level flight under operational conditions, the Hurricane mounted four Brownings in each wing and was powered by a Rolls-Royce Merlin engine. And with its rate of climb of better than 2000 ft/min (610 m/min) the Hurricane at last offered the possibility of mounting an effective defence against attacks by the new generation of high-speed bombers.

This was an important development. In 1934 it had been concluded by a committee set up to investigate the problem that the increasing speed of bombers was presenting the fighters designed to intercept them with an almost impossible problem: enemy bombers crossing the coast of Britain at a height of 10,000 ft (3048 m) or more and a speed of over 200 mph (322 km/h) would have reached their targets in London or the Midlands before the fighters could get within range. In the absence of a warning system to provide advance notice of the bombers' approach, the only way to intercept them would be to maintain standing patrols of fighters, and given the length of coastline it would be necessary to patrol, this was bound to be an impossibly costly system to maintain. Coupled with the government's policy of achieving parity with the Luftwaffe – initially taken to mean simple equality of numbers, and later amended to indicate an equivalent striking power – the emphasis continued to be on the provision of more bombers at the expense of fighters.

However, in December 1937 a different strategy began to take shape. The Air Staff had been asked to provide estimates for the strength necessary to counter the threat from Germany, and their response was a predictable recommendation for more squadrons of bigger bombers. This was rejected by Sir Thomas Inskip, who in March 1936 had been appointed Minister for the Co-ordination of Defence: instead, Inskip suggested that the best defence against German bombing attacks would be defensive fighters rather than bombers. His reasoning was that Germany was not in a position to fight a long war any more than Britain was in a position to win a short one, and that it might be sounder policy to take advantage of Germany's weakness. With the new fighters now in production, and, equally importantly, with the aid of the early warning provided by the new radar equipment,

it would at last be possible to mount an effective defence against bomber attacks.

Accordingly, it was decided to concentrate on building up fighter reserves, and during 1938 the Hurricane was joined in production by a second new fighter, the Supermarine Spitfire. Also based on the Merlin engine and armed with eight wing-mounted Brownings, the Spitfire was of considerably more modern design than the Hurricane, using stressed-skin construction. Whereas the Hurricane carried its guns close to the fuselage with the undercarriage retracting inwards, the Spitfire reversed the process, with a narrow-track undercarriage retracting outwards towards the wingtips and the guns carried further outboard in the distinctive broad-chord elliptical wings. In combination, the two types formed an excellent partnership: the Hurricane was more straightforward to build, so that large numbers could be provided relatively quickly, while the Spitfire, requiring considerably more work in the manufacturing process, offered correspondingly higher performance and an astonishing capacity for improvement.

The second vital component of the air defence system, the radio detection equipment (radar), was also in an advanced stage of development by 1938. The first exercise to test the technique of ground controlled interception (GCI) during 1936 had produced such promising results that work was started on building a string of radar stations known as Chain Home, which were later supplemented by Chain Home Low stations to guard against the approach of low-flying aircraft. By the beginning of 1938 fighters from Biggin Hill in Kent were being directed by the original station at Bawdsey, in Suffolk, to intercept airliners approaching Croydon airport from the continent.

At the same time, a system of operational control was being developed. From the individual stations, reports were transmitted to Bentley Priory, near Stanmore in Middlesex, where Air Chief Marshal Sir Hugh Dowding, Commander-in-Chief of Fighter Command, had his headquarters. Here the reports from the various stations were compared and evaluated in the Filter Room, before the positions of attacking and defending aircraft were plotted on a map table for transmission to the various operations rooms that were established at the headquarters of each Fighter Group as well as at Fighter Command HQ. In September 1938 there were two groups, No 11 with 19 squadrons and No 12 with 12, the former concentrated south of Bedford and the latter extending north of Bedford as far as York.

Another component of Fighter Command was No 30 Balloon Group, whose 10 squadrons in London,

A Canadian built Hurricane IIB preserved by the Strathallan Collection

Surrey, Middlesex and Essex were deployed during
the Munich crisis in September 1938. A few weeks
later, on 1 November, No 30 became Balloon Command, and during the next year a further three groups
were formed. No 31 included seven squadrons based
around Birmingham, five around Manchester, three
around Liverpool and one in the Derby area. No 32
included three squadrons defending Bristol, two each
for Portsmouth and Southampton and one for Cardiff,
and No 33 included three squadrons each allocated
to Newcastle-upon-Tyne, Hull, Sheffield and Glasgow. The number of balloons each squadron operated
varied from 16 to 45; they were deployed from light
trucks or, in coastal areas, barges, and their job was to
create barriers of steel cables suspended from the balloons to force attacking aircraft to fly higher than the
5000 ft (1524 m) or so to which the balloons were set,
thus bringing them within range of the anti-aircraft
guns and discouraging low-level attacks.

Earlier that year, too, the rapid build-up of equipment for the growing number of squadrons was
reflected in the formation of Maintenance Command.
This organisation took over responsibility for all
supply depots. The potential for aircraft production
was expanded by the establishment of facilities in
Canada, as well as by orders placed with manufacturers in the United States, both of which would
become important sources of new aircraft.

Meanwhile, the new emphasis on defence did not
mean that the supply of new types of bomber had
ceased. A 1932 specification for a twin-engined day
bomber to carry a 1000-lb (454-kg) bombload over a
range of 720 miles (1159 km) and with a maximum
range of 1500 miles (2414 km) resulted in two new
types, first of which was the Handley Page Hampden.
The Hampden entered service in September 1938 and
proved capable of delivering a 4000-lb (1814-kg) load
of bombs, but despite its makers' claims for it as a
'fighter bomber', and the provision of a fixed forward-
firing machine gun, the defensive armament of single
hand-held machine guns in nose, dorsal and ventral
positions proved completely inadequate.

The second bomber resulting from the same specification joined No 9 Squadron the following February.
This was the Vickers Wellington, which, like the
Wellesley, was constructed using the geodetic system.
Unlike the Wellesley, however, it had an internal
bomb bay big enough for nine 500-lb (227-kg) bombs,
which it could carry for 2000 miles (3219 km), and
with a similar number of 250-lb (113-kg) bombs the
range was extended to 3000 miles (4828 km). Armament comprised twin Brownings in powered nose and
tail turrets, and early examples also had a retractable
ventral turret, though this was soon abandoned.

The Wellington was the last new bomber to join
Bomber Command before the outbreak of war in
September 1939, by which time it was in service with
all eight squadrons of No 3 Group as well as two squadrons of No 6 Group. The remainder of No 6 comprised five squadrons of Battles, three of Blenheims and

two each of Hampdens and Whitleys. While No 3 was an operational group, with two of its squadrons being reserve units, No 6 was engaged in operational training.

No 1 Group Bomber Command at this time consisted of 10 squadrons of Battles, and following the order for mobilisation of all RAF units on 23 August No 1 was reconstituted as the Advanced Air Striking Force. The AASF was in turn divided into five wings, Nos 71, 72, 74, 75 and 76, of two squadrons each, and on 2 September, in accordance with existing plans, these flew to French bases in the Rheims area, a matter of hours before England and France declared war on Germany.

No 2 Group was equipped with Blenheims, with six operational and one reserve squadron divided into Nos 82, 83 and 79 Wings. No 4 Group's six squadrons of Whitleys included one reserve squadron, and No 5's eight squadrons of Whitleys included two reserve squadrons. Thus Bomber Command's home-based operational strength amounted to six squadrons each of Blenheims, Wellingtons and Whitleys and Hampdens, and five of Whitleys.

Fighter Command, in the year since the Munich agreement, had reached a position of much greater strength. All the Furys and Demons, and the bulk of the Gauntlets, had been replaced by Hurricanes, Spitfires and Blenheims, though there were still four squadrons of Gladiators. The formation or mobilisation of an additional eight squadrons had enabled a new group, No 10, to be formed for the protection of the southwest of the country.

Coastal Command was rather less well equipped. Its three groups, No 18 based in Scotland, No 16 in southeastern England and No 15 covering western England and the Irish Sea, disposed of a total of 19 squadrons, including six of flying boats. The land-based reconnaissance squadrons included 10 of Ansons and two of Vildebeests, both of which were obsolescent by this stage, and only one squadron was equipped with the new Lockheed Hudson that had been ordered in 1938 by the first purchasing mission to the United

Below: A Vickers Wellington X after post-war conversion for training duties

An Avro Manchester prepares for take-off, with a Vickers Wellington in the distance

States. Based on the Lockheed Super Electra, an 11-seat passenger aircraft, the Hudson was powered by a pair of 1100-hp Wright Cyclone radial engines and armed with twin Brownings in a powered dorsal turret.

Coastal Command's flying boat squadrons were hardly better off. One squadron was still flying Stranraers, and another three were equipped with Saunders-Roe Londons, the latter being twin-engined biplanes that were clearly obsolescent. One of the London squadrons, however, was in the process of converting to Sunderlands, which also formed the equipment of the remaining two flying-boat squadrons.

The Short Sunderland was developed from the Short C Class Empire passenger flying boat in the mid-1930s, and was a four-engined all-metal monoplane. It was armed with powered turrets in the bow and stern, the former with a single Browning and the latter with four, plus single manually aimed Vickers K guns on each side of the beam, while up to 2000 lb (907 kg) of bombs, depth charges or mines could be carried. With its long range and roomy interior the Sunderland was to prove highly adaptable, serving principally as a convoy escort and maritime patrol aircraft, but also proving useful for air-sea rescue and emergency transport and claiming an impressive number of victims in aerial combat.

The army co-operation squadrons were in an equally poor state. In addition to two squadrons of Blenheims and four of Hurricanes which had been allocated to form part of the Air Component, British Expeditionary Force, there were five operational and two reserve squadrons in existence in August 1939. One of the reserve squadrons was still using Hawker Hinds, and the other Hawker Hectors, another Hart derivative produced as an interim replacement for the Audax.

The remaining five army co-operation squadrons were by now standardised on the Westland Lysander, a two-seat high-wing monoplane with fixed undercarriage that had been designed to meet a specification issued in 1935. The undercarriage fairings each accommodated a Browning machine gun, whose ammunition was fed through the fairings from boxes in the fuselage, and stub wings could be fitted to allow up to 500 lb (227 kg) of bombs to be carried. The observer in the rear of the enclosed cockpit had the time-honoured single Lewis gun, though this was later replaced by twin Brownings, and the outstanding quality of the Lysander was its very low minimum flying speed of 59 mph (95 km/h). Its top speed was 229 mph (368 km/h), and the makers' optimistic suggestion that the Lysander's low-flying qualities might enable it to out-manoeuvre faster enemy fighters was unfortunately not borne out by experience.

While the deteriorating situation in Europe had focussed attention on home defence and the build-up of the bomber force at home, the RAF still had considerable overseas commitments. Egypt remained the centre of activities in the Middle East, and the RAF Command there included five squadrons of Blenheims, three of Gladiators, two of Valentia bomber transports and one each of Lysanders and Wellesleys. In addition, the Sudan Wing comprised a squadron of Wellesleys based at Nairobi and another of mixed Wellesleys and Vincents at Khartoum. A single squadron based at Ramleh came under the Palestine and Transjordan Command, and this included Hardys, Gauntlets and Lysanders on its strength. British Forces in Iraq had been reduced to a single squadron of Blenheims at Shaibah, while the Aden Command comprised one squadron of Vincents and Blenheims, a second of Gladiators and a third of Singapore flying boats. Another squadron of London flying boats was based on Malta, but immediately after the outbreak of war this was moved to Gibraltar.

Trenchard's plan for the RAF to take over military

control in India had never been put into effect, so the six squadrons there were equipped mainly for army co-operation work. Apart from one squadron of Blenheims and another equipped with Harts and Tiger Moths for training purposes, there were two squadrons of Audaxes and one of Wapitis, plus a bomber transport squadron with Valentias.

Singapore, on the other hand, was regarded as essentially a naval base, since an overland attack through the jungles of Malaya was considered impossible, and the main defences were composed of artillery batteries. These were supplemented by two squadrons of Vildebeest torpedo bombers and two of reconnaissance flying boats, which in August 1939 were equipped with Singapores and Sunderlands. During that month, two squadrons of Blenheims arrived from India to reinforce the colony, and another two Blenheim squadrons were despatched from Britain, arriving during September. Another squadron of Vildebeests

based in Ceylon (Sri Lanka) completed RAF Far East Command.

Following the signing of the non-aggression treaty between Germany and the Soviet Union on 23 August 1939, the RAF reserves were mobilised and the force put on a war footing. Two days later the Anglo-Polish treaty of mutual assistance was signed and on 1 September Germany invaded Poland. On 3 September, acting on instructions from London, the British ambassador in Germany delivered an ultimatum calling on Germany to cease hostilities against Poland by 11.00 am. The deadline passed without response from Hitler, and Britain, followed by France, declared war on Germany. The RAF was 21 years old, and for the second time it was involved in a world war. For most of the preceding 20 years of peace it had been on active service somewhere in the world, but now it would be called on to fight over land and sea around the globe.

Wartime scene at a flying boat base, with a Short Sunderland III on the slipway

6 THE DEFENSIVE WAR

Within minutes of the prime minister's announcement that Britain was at war with Germany, the air raid sirens sounded over London: an unidentified aircraft had been plotted approaching from the continent. It was soon established that this was nothing more than a French aircraft carrying the assistant air attaché, but three days later there was a more serious alarm.

This time the report came from a searchlight crew in the Thames estuary, and as fighters scrambled to meet the threat they appeared on the radar screens as a growing force of aircraft out to sea. The result was more fighters being ordered into the air, which only added to the confusion, and it was some time before the mistake was realised.

The state of edgy alertness which characterised these incidents was a result of the growing fear of air attack over the previous decade. Almost everyone, whether taking Trenchard's view that the only effective response was the capacity for retaliatory raids, or accepting the idea that fighter defences were the essential requirement, believed that Germany would attempt to knock out Britain by an immediate, all-out aerial bombardment. To that extent, while the false alarms were disturbing, there was some reassurance to be gained from the swiftness of the response.

However, as the weeks passed, it became clear that there was to be no immediate assault on Britain. At the same time, the British bombers were inhibited by political considerations from beginning any full-scale offensive of their own: the French were reluctant to allow such provocative action from continental bases, and the limited range of the bombers available would not allow them to reach targets in Germany without violating Dutch and Belgian neutrality. As it happened, Germany was not in any position to mount a full-scale bombing offensive in any case, since the Luftwaffe had been built up as a tactical air force to support army operations.

Consequently, most of the early air engagements took place at sea, as reconnaissance aircraft encountered each other, anti-shipping strikes were intercepted, and Bomber Command's activities were limited to the dropping of propaganda leaflets and sporadic attacks on German warships. The most immediate problem remained the air force in France.

The RAF was committed to supporting the British Expeditionary Force's 10 divisions in France, and following the arrival of the Advanced Air Striking Force on the day before the declaration of war, four squadrons of Hurricanes and two of Blenheims arrived within the next few days. Four army co-operation squadrons of Lysanders and another two of Blenheims had arrived by the end of October, and in December another two Blenheim squadrons joined them. In that month all the RAF units were incorporated in a new command, British Air Forces in France, under the operational control of the BEF. There were continuing demands for more fighter squadrons, though these were strenuously resisted by Dowding at Fighter Command, whose efforts were concentrated on building up adequate air defences, and who refused to allow any Spitfire squadrons to be based across the Channel.

With the exception of a fifth squadron of Lysanders which joined the BAFF in April 1940, the units that had arrived by the end of December constituted the total RAF force in France until the German invasion began in May. Again, they were limited in their operations both by the French desire to avoid provocation and by the lack of existing facilities, and reconnaissance continued to be their main task until the German Blitzkrieg was launched.

Meanwhile, in April 1940 the German forces occupied Denmark and launched an invasion of Norway in order to pre-empt British plans to mine Norwegian waters and hinder the supply of Swedish iron ore to Germany. Two squadrons of fighters, No 263 with Gladiators and No 46 with Hurricanes, were sent to Norway and these provided some measure of fighter cover. Many of the Gladiators were destroyed on the frozen lake from which they were operating by German bomber attacks, and the surviving fighters were lost following evacuation, when the carrier HMS *Glorious* on which they had embarked was sunk.

By this time the invasion of France was almost over. A further four Hurricane squadrons had been sent to France almost as soon as the fighting began, but the position was hopeless from the start. The Battles and Blenheims were no match for the German fighters – in one raid alone, on 14 May, more than half of a force of 67 Blenheims and Battles were lost in attacks on

Far left: The crew of a Bristol Blenheim I emerge from their aircraft after a flight

Previous spread: Supermarine Spitfire II

Left: Servicing a Westland Lysander in the snow on a French airfield

Above: Fairey Battles prepare to take off from a snow-covered airfield

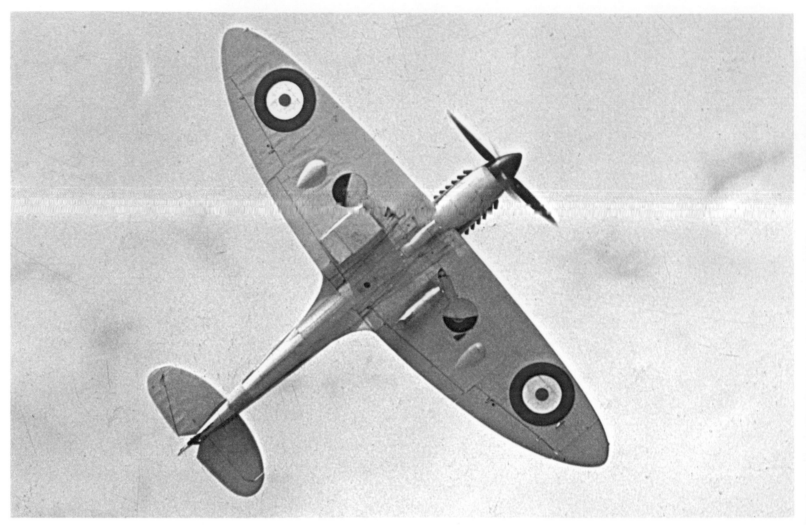

One of the enduring symbols of the Battle of Britain: the elliptical wings of a Spitfire in flight

bridges and other targets in the area around Sedan – and within a matter of days the army co-operation squadrons were being withdrawn, leaving the bulk of their aircraft behind, either victims of the fighting or destroyed for lack of fuel or equipment.

The AASF squadrons, meanwhile, had been by-passed by the main German advance, and it proved almost impossible to redeploy them. The fighters were in constant action, claiming many victories, but there was inevitable attrition. Altogether, a total of 959 RAF aircraft were lost during May and June, including 432 fighters. Most of the latter were Hurricanes, though there had also been losses among the Spitfire squadrons covering the evacuation of the BEF from Dunkirk, flying at the limit of their range from bases in southeast England. At the same time a high proportion of the 1284 Luftwaffe aircraft lost had been victims of the British fighters.

The evacuation from Dunkirk was completed on 4 June, and on 18 June the last squadrons in France were withdrawn to England. The Luftwaffe was now able to operate from captured bases in northern France, and with the severe depletion of the fighter squadrons that had taken place, the German bombers now constituted a much more serious threat to Britain. Almost half of the total of operational fighters had been lost during May and June, and only record production by the aircraft factories during the months of June and July, when a total of 942 new Spitfires and Hurricanes were delivered, enabled Fighter

Command to prepare for the battle that would now take place in the skies over southern England.

In the meantime, German air attacks were concentrated on shipping in the Channel, as preparations for the seaborne invasion of Britain were put in hand. Fighter Command, meanwhile, was being strengthened and reorganised, and by the end of the first week in August it consisted of four groups and a total of 56 squadrons. Among these, however, were six squadrons of the improvised and largely ineffective Blenheim IFs, another squadron which consisted of a single flight of Gladiators, and two more equipped with the Boulton Paul Defiant.

The Defiant was the successor to the two-seater Demon fighters. Produced in response to a 1935 specification, it was armed with four Browning machine guns carried in a powered turret and intended to fly standing patrols, using its guns to attack bombers from below. The first squadron deliveries were not made until December 1939, however, by which time the whole concept had become outmoded: lack of familiarity on the part of German pilots enabled some early successes to be achieved, but as soon as the type's lack of forward-firing guns was appreciated it became easy prey as a day interceptor, and was switched to night fighting.

By August, there were no Defiants left in No 11 Group, whose 13 squadrons of Hurricanes, six of Spitfires and two of Blenheims were based at 13 airfields in the southeast of the country. No 10 Group,

BRITISH AIRFIELDS, 1940

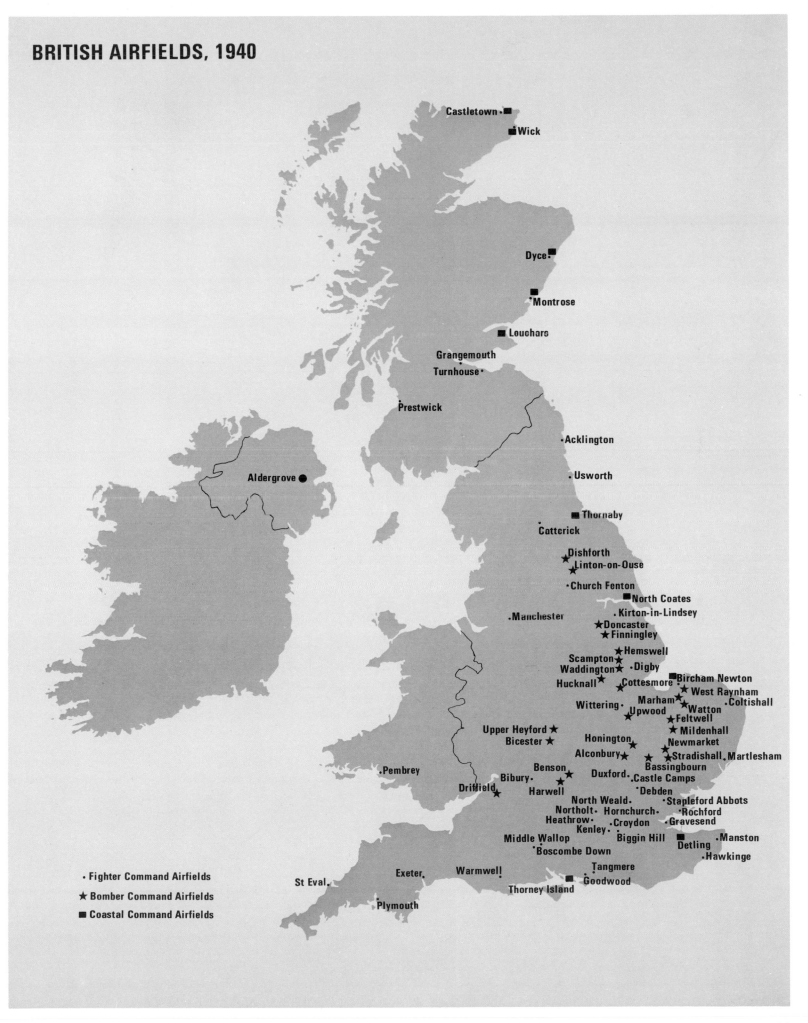

Castletown · ▪ Wick

Dyce ·

▪ Montrose

▪ Lougharo

Grangemouth
Turnhouse ·

Prestwick

· Acklington

Aldergrove ●

· Usworth

▪ Thornaby
· Catterick

★ Dishforth
★ Linton-on-Ouse

· Church Fenton

▪ North Coates

· Manchester

· Kirton-in-Lindsey

★ Doncaster
★ Finningley

★ Hemswell

Scampton ·
Waddington ★ · Digby

Hucknall ★ · Cottesmore ▪ Bircham Newton
★ West Raynham

Wittering · Marham ★ · Coltishall
★ · Watton
Upwood · · Feltwell

Upper Heyford ★ ★ · Mildenhall
Bicester · ★ Honington ★ · Newmarket

Alconbury ★ ★ · Stradishall · Martlesham

Benson ★ Duxford · · Bassingbourn

Pembrey ·

Bibury · · Castle Camps
Driffield · Harwell ★ · Debden

North Weald · · Stapleford Abbots
Northolt · Hornchurch · · Rochford
Heathrow · · Croydon · Gravesend
Kenley ·

Middle Wallop · Biggin Hill ▪ Detling · Manston
Boscombe Down · · Hawkinge

Exeter · Warmwell · · Tangmere
St Eval · Thorney Island · Goodwood

Plymouth ·

· Fighter Command Airfields
★ Bomber Command Airfields
▪ Coastal Command Airfields

Pilots of No 111 Squadron race to their Hawker Hurricanes during the battle for France, May 1940

whose territory was southwestern England and South Wales, comprised four squadrons of Spitfires, three of Hurricanes, and single squadrons of Gladiators and Blenheims, the Gladiator unit being only one flight. No 12 Group, with responsibility for the defence of the Midlands, disposed of six squadrons of Spitfires, five of Hurricanes, two of Blenheims and one of Defiants, while to the north of the Humber and the Mersey No 13 Group consisted of nine Hurricane, two Spitfire, one Defiant and one Blenheim squadrons.

With such limited resources, the key to success would be their efficient employment, and in this respect the system that had been built up in the five years of Fighter Command's existence was to prove decisive. Warning of the approach of German bomber formations was provided by the coastal radar stations, and after they had crossed the coast they were tracked by the network of Observer Corps posts. Reports from these were analysed and co-ordinated in the Filter Room at Bentley Priory. The resulting situation reports were duplicated on the Operations Room plotting tables at Fighter Command and Group headquarters, and from the Group the information was

passed to the appropriate Sector Operations Room. Each sector was a division of the group, and it was at the sector headquarters that operational control of the squadrons within the sector, and of units in the air, was exercised. After receiving the order to take-off, the pilots were guided to their targets by the sector controllers.

In their efforts, the Fighter Command pilots were assisted by tactical and operational miscalculations on the part of the Luftwaffe. The German bombers were armed with hand-aimed machine guns which proved inevitably inadequate for defence, so that the German fighters were restricted to providing close escorts for the bombers. Thus the Bf 109 pilots, whose machines were in many respects superior to the opposing Hurricanes and Spitfires, were often left to watch in relative helplessness as RAF fighters dived past them to attack the bombers. The Bf 109s, too, were fighting at the limit of their range, while the long-range Bf 110s proved ineffective fighters.

As far as the Luftwaffe was concerned, the Battle of Britain, intended to be the preliminary to the cross-channel invasion, fell into four distinct phases. Following the attacks on Allied shipping in the Channel, which by 25 July succeeded in discouraging any further attempts to send convoys through the Straits of Dover in daylight, there was an attempt to lure the British fighters into the air and destroy them. On 8 August the effort was switched to a bombing offensive against the fighter bases themselves, with supplementary raids on aircraft factories. By the end of the first week of September Fighter Command losses were rapidly outstripping the rate of replacements, but at this point the German offensive was turned against London, and for three weeks daylight raids on the capital were mounted.

The change of emphasis was, to a large extent, the salvation of Fighter Command. Free to operate without the interference of continual attacks on their bases, the Hurricanes and Spitfires were able to blunt the attacks on London, claiming large numbers of bombers destroyed and, in the end, forcing the Luftwaffe to turn to night attacks. More important, the plan to invade Britain, which in turn depended on the destruction of the RAF's fighters, had to be postponed indefinitely.

Combatting the night raids called for new tactics and, before it could be done effectively, new aircraft and new equipment. The Blenheims that had been hopefully fitted out for the task were too slow and too lightly armed to carry out effective interceptions. However, they played an important part in the development of the airborne interception radar that was the main requirement, mainly because they had room to accommodate the bulky equipment and its operator. The first AI radar-equipped Blenheims had begun trials shortly before the outbreak of war, and by April 1940 all six of Fighter Command's Blenheim squadrons were using the new device.

The first success using AI radar was achieved on the night of 22/23 July 1940, but subsequent victories were rare until the Blenheims were replaced by Bristol Beaufighters during the second half of 1940. The Beaufighter was big and heavy, but with two 1560-hp Bristol Hercules engines it was capable of 320 mph (515 km/h), and it carried a heavy armament of four 20-mm Hispano cannon in the nose plus six Brownings in the wings. No radar was fitted until November, by which time five of the six Blenheim squadrons had made the conversion to the new type, but the Mk IV that was then fitted in place of the Mk III equipment used on the Blenheim night fighters was considerably more effective. The first kill came on 11 November, but it was not until January 1941, when GCI equipment that could track both interceptor and quarry became operational, that a useful rate of success began to be achieved.

Three victories for the Beaufighters in that first month were followed by a steadily mounting toll, with 22 kills in March eclipsed by a total of 48 in April and no fewer than 96 in the first 10 days of May. The efforts of the Beaufighters were supplemented by Blenheims carrying out night intruder missions against the bombers' bases, waiting for them to return from the raids and attacking them as they neared home. The last of the major night raids on London was made on the night of 10/11 May 1941, following which the bulk of the Luftwaffe was withdrawn from the bombing offensive against England, to concentrate on the build-up for the German invasion of the Soviet Union.

May 1941 also saw the flight of the first night-fighter version of one of the outstanding aircraft of the war, the De Havilland Mosquito. The Mosquito brought a new level of performance to the job, being capable of almost 50 mph (80 km/h) more than the

De Havilland Mosquito NF.2 night fighters, showing the nose aerials for the airborne interception radar

Beaufighter. The further addition of the AI Mk VIII radar, operating at much shorter wavelengths and able to scan the sky ahead, made the NF.XII version of the Mosquito, which joined the original NF.II in service during 1942 the leading Allied night fighter of the war.

AI radar was not the only night fighting aid to be introduced in the early stages of the war. During 1940 numbers of Douglas DB-7 Havocs were received from the United States, and a small proportion of these had the glazed bomber nose replaced by solid noses housing batteries of eight or 12 machine guns plus AI radar sets. The first squadron to be equipped with Havoc night fighters was No 85, which began operations with the type in February 1940 and continued until the following September.

In fact, No 85 was the only squadron to use the Havoc as a normal night fighter, and other examples were used in less conventional ways. In December 1940 No 93 Squadron was formed to use another variant of the Havoc, which was fitted with a device known as the Long Aerial Mine, or alternatively by the code name Pandora. This consisted of 2000 ft (610 m) of piano wire, at the end of which was attached a small explosive charge. Wire and charge were either trailed behind the aircraft, or released on small parachutes. In fact it created more of a hazard to the parent aircraft than to any opponent.

The dangers of the Pandora led to its abandonment, and instead Havocs were switched to Turbinlite squadrons. The idea behind these units was that the Havocs, or Bostons as some models were known, with 2,700,000,000-candlepower searchlights in the nose, would home in on hostile bombers, then switch on the searchlight to illuminate the target for accompanying Hurricanes to shoot down. No fewer than nine Turbinlite squadrons were formed in September 1942, with 70 Havocs modified to carry the searchlights, but by January 1943 only two hostile and one friendly aircraft had been successfully attacked using the system, while 17 Havocs had been lost in crashes, and the squadrons were disbanded.

Mosquito bombers with their crews preparing for a mission in February 1943

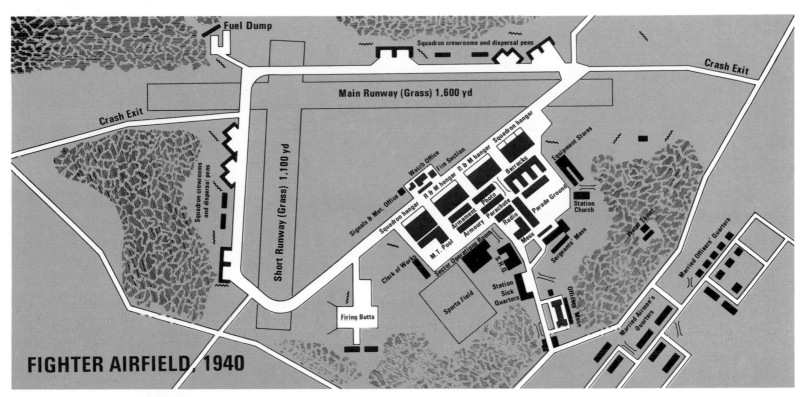

FIGHTER AIRFIELD, 1940

Labels: Fuel Dump; Squadron crewrooms and dispersal pens; Crash Exit; Main Runway (Grass) 1,600 yd; Crash Exit; Short Runway (Grass) 1,100 yd; Squadron crewrooms and dispersal pens; Watch Office; Fire Section; R & M hangar; R & M hangar; Squadron hangar; Equipment Stores; Signals & Met. Office; Squadron hangar; Armament; Photo; Parachute; Barracks; Radio; Parade Ground; Station Church; Clerk of Works; M.T. Pool; Armoury; Mess; Sergeants Mess; Water Tower; Married Officers' Quarters; Sector Operations Room; S.H.O.; Officers' Mess; Married Airmen's Quarters; Sports Field; Station Sick Quarters; Firing Butts

The Bristol Beaufighter proved an ideal vehicle for the early airborne interception radar equipment

An early example of the Douglas DB-7 imported from the United States and used both as a night fighter, under the name Havoc, and as a light bomber, in which role it was known as the Boston

A variety of inducements are
offered to potential volunteers in
the window of this recruiting office
in the spring of 1941

7 THE BOMBING OFFENSIVE

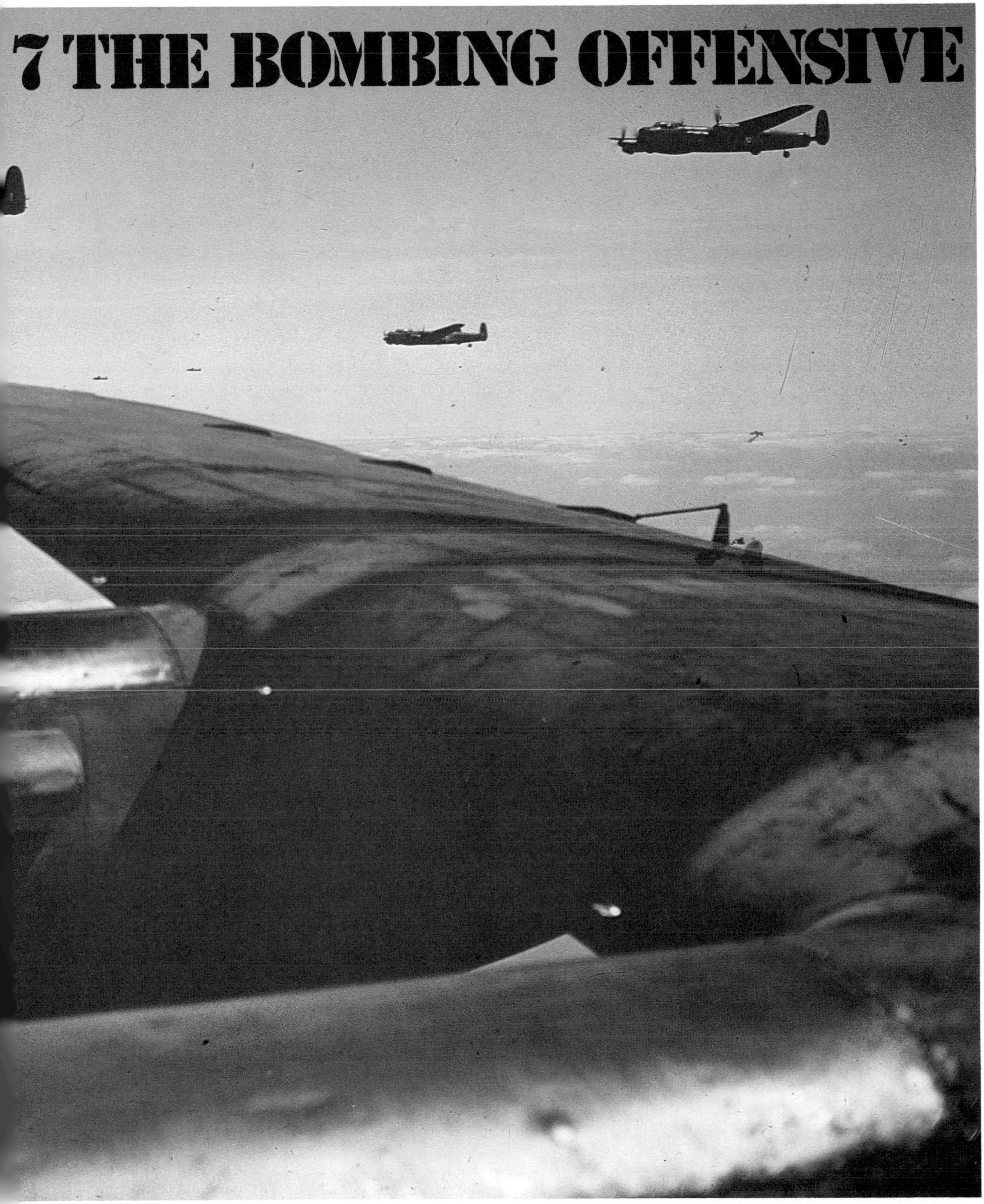

The principal effect of the leaflet-dropping and anti-shipping raids that constituted Bomber Command's main activities during the early part of the war was to demonstrate the ineffectiveness of the equipment at its disposal. The bombers proved vulnerable to the German fighters, being inadequately armed and unprotected by armour or self-sealing fuel tanks; navigation by night was still a matter of star sights and uncertain radio beacons backing up dead reckoning; and systems were prone to malfunction or would seize up altogether in the extreme cold encountered at high altitudes, where the crews also became liable to frostbite and oxygen starvation. It was unsafe for the bombers to operate by day, while at night they had little chance of even finding their targets, let alone delivering their bombs accurately.

During the first eight months of the war the bombers were in any case held back from attacks on Germany. However, following the invasion of France and the German bombing of Rotterdam, while No 2 Group's Blenheims joined the attacks on German communications and troop concentrations, suffering losses almost as heavy as those of the French-based Blenheims and Battles, the first raids were mounted on targets in Germany.

A camouflaged Fairey Battle on a
French airfield in 1940. The
crippling losses suffered by Battles
and Blenheims in daylight raids in
the early stages of the war were one
of the factors behind the switch to
the night bombing offensive

In April the priority of targets to be attacked had
been defined as oil installations in the Ruhr, railway
marshalling yards (harassing action only) and, where
these could not be located, 'any self-illuminating or
identifiable targets': coke ovens were quoted as an
example of the last. Bomber Command was of the
opinion that only 50 per cent of average crews would
be capable of locating a target at night in good visi-
bility and where there was some conspicuous aid to
help them, such as a coastline or river, and that in the
absence of such aids very few crews would be capable
of finding it at all.

This opinion was borne out by the results of the
first attack on the Ruhr oil refineries on the night of
15 May. Out of 78 Wellingtons, Whitleys and Hampdens of Nos 3, 4 and 5 Groups, only 24 claimed to have
found the designated targets, and while losses were
minimal and substantial damage was caused to the
marshalling yards in several places later estimates of
the accuracy of the raids concluded that, on average,
only one in 10 of the aircraft reported to have attacked
specific targets in the Ruhr had been within five miles
of its target.

Clearly, there was a great deal of room for improvement: in the meantime, the emphasis was switched to
the destruction of the invasion barges which were
being assembled at Dutch and Belgian ports. This was
accomplished much more effectively, and a raid on
Berlin on 25 August also had satisfactory results, not
in the negligible damage inflicted but in the subsequent switch of the German bomber offensive away
from the Fighter Command bases to London and other
cities.

By the end of 1940 it was becoming clear that
precision bombing of industrial and military targets
was possible, but only with very high loss rate for the
crews involved. Moonlight and a readily identifiable
target were essential, and to hit the target the bomber
needed to fly straight and level for as much as 10 miles.
Since important targets were likely to be well defended,
such an approach was verging on the suicidal, and it
was eventually decided that since most of the bombs
would miss anyway, the answer lay in more extensive
bombing of a whole area. At the same time there was a
requirement for more effective bombs, and for more
accurate methods of assessing the damage caused.

By this stage more effective bombers were beginning
to arrive, though several promising designs were com-
promised to a greater or lesser extent by the terms of
the original specification. The Short Stirling, for
example, was built to meet a 1936 specification calling
for a four-engined heavy bomber capable of 230 mph
(370 km/h) at 15,000 ft (4572 m) with a range of at
least 3000 miles (4827 km), a service ceiling of 28,000 ft
(8534 m) with a 2000-lb (907-kg) bombload and all-
round defensive armament. The overall limiting
factor on the design, however, was the stipulation of a
maximum wing span of 100 ft (31 m), to allow the new
bomber to fit through the standard hangar door
width.

The result was that the wings were of long chord
with a corresponding low aspect ratio, in order to
obtain the necessary area, so that performance at
altitude was severely restricted and a fully loaded
Stirling was pushed to get above 12,000 ft (3658 m).
The tall undercarriage dictated by the high wing
position made ground handling tricky, and the
Stirling was very slow in climbing. The two-gun nose
and dorsal turrets and four-guns in the tail formed a
useful defensive armament, and at the time it entered
service in August 1940 it was the RAF's only four-
engined bomber. A divided bomb bay meant that the
biggest bomb that could be carried was 4000 lb (1814
kg), but 24 500-lb (227-kg) bombs could be carried
without using the auxiliary fuel tanks, and up to a
total of 14,000 lb (6350 kg) over shorter ranges.

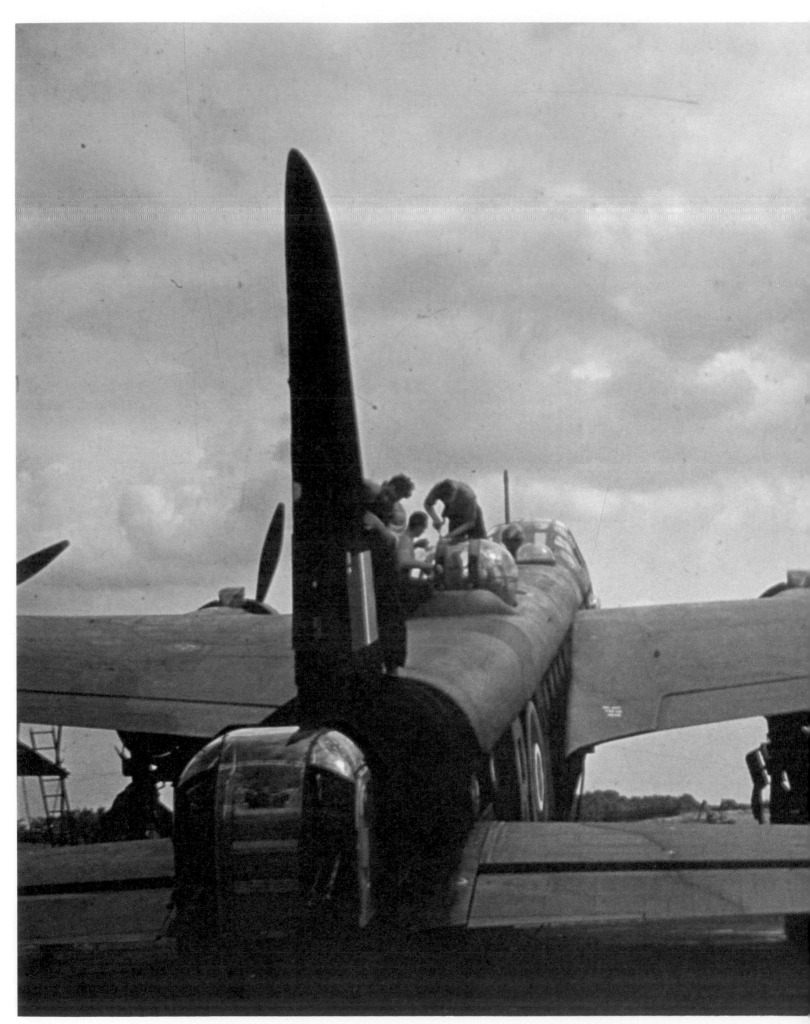

BOMBER STATION, 1940

22
No 1
18
No 6
6124 ft
11   No 5   4383 ft
4120 ft   No 2   29
Control Tower
No 4   No 3   Camp Buildings
04   36

Ground crews at work on Short
Stirlings of No 149 Squadron at
RAF Mildenhall, late 1941. The
Stirling was the principal heavy
bomber in the early stages of the
bombing offensive against Germany

The RAF's other four-engined bombers both began life as twin-engined types using the Rolls-Royce Vulture engine stipulated by another specification of 1936. The Avro Manchester actually entered service with this powerplant in November 1940, but this otherwise outstanding design was ruined by the completely unreliable engines, and production was abandoned after the first 200 or so had been completed.

The Handley Page design to the same specification was abandoned at an early stage, and the Vickers-Armstrong Warwick was redesigned to use Bristol Centaurus then Pratt & Whitney Double Wasp radials, but by the time the first production example was flown in May 1942 the design was out of date, and most Warwicks were used as transport, reconnaissance or air-sea rescue aircraft.

In the meantime, the original Handley Page twin-Vulture design had been enlarged to use four Merlin engines, and in this form the first prototype was flown in October 1939. By the time production examples were entering service alongside Manchesters in November 1940 the Halifax, as the new type was named, was armed with two-gun nose and four-gun tail turrets, plus a single Browning on each side of the beam. Halifaxes ultimately served in a variety of roles apart from night bombing, and in the Mediterranean and Far Eastern theatres as well as with Bomber Command in Europe.

Performance of the early Halifax models was not particularly impressive, but the installation of 1650-hp Bristol Hercules XVI sleeve-valve radials in the Mk III improved matters. The 1800-hp Hercules 100 fitted to the Mk VI from 1944 raised the maximum speed to 311 mph (501 km/h). Range with a 13,000-lb (5897-kg) bombload was 1077 miles (1734 km), and in 75,532 bombing sorties Bomber Command Halifaxes dropped a total of 227,610 tons (231,251,760 kg) of bombs. This represented more than twice the total weight delivered by Wellingtons in just under double the number of sorties, but the Halifax's totals were

more than doubled again by the most famous of all Bomber Command's aircraft, the Avro Lancaster.

The Lancaster was derived from the Manchester by a process similar to that which produced the Halifax, namely by replacing the two Vultures with four Merlins. Apart from the new wing centre sections demanded by the new powerplant, the basic Manchester airframe remained substantially unchanged, and many of the early Lancasters used original Manchester fuselages. Among the many attributes of the resulting bomber was an ability to deliver its bombs from a height of 20,000 ft, a much safer altitude than that of the Stirling, whose crews suffered many anxious minutes on bomb runs as the Lancasters and Halifaxes rained their bombs down from thousands of feet above. Another safety factor was the Lancaster's ability to stay airborne on only two engines, and to absorb substantial damage, and this was reflected in the type's low loss rate: while one Stirling was lost for every 41 tons (41,656 kg) of bombs dropped, and one

Halifax for every 56 tons (56,896 kg), the average for the Lancaster was 132 tons (134,112 kg). One Lancaster managed 140 operational sorties, compared with an average for the type of around 20.

By January 1942 Bomber Command was a formidable organisation. No 1 Group had nine Wellington squadrons operational and one in reserve, while the other group principally equipped with Wellingtons, No 3, had 10 operational and one in reserve, as well as three squadrons operational with Stirlings. Most of the Wellingtons in service at this stage were Mk ICs, which dispensed with the ventral turret in favour of beam guns. Other later models of the Wellington included the Mks II, III and IV, powered by, respectively, Merlin, Hercules and Twin Wasp engines, while the last Bomber Command variant was the Hercules-powered Mk X.

No 2 Group at this stage was still mainly equipped with Blenheims, which equipped six of its operational squadrons. Another was already operational with

A Lancaster prepares to take off on a night mission from that familiar wartime location, 'somewhere in England'

Inset: The Lancaster's forerunner, the Avro Manchester, was the victim of its unsuccessful Vulture engines. This example belonged to No 207 Squadron

Bostons, another was in the process of conversion, while a third was converting to Mosquito Mk IVs. The Boston was the basic light bomber version of the Douglas DB-7, also used by Fighter Command as a night fighter with the name Havoc. The B.IV was the first main bomber version of the De Havilland Mosquito, the most versatile RAF aircraft of the war and Bomber Command's fastest bomber for nearly 10 years.

Originally built as a private venture light bomber, the Mosquito was designed to be built entirely of wood, following established De Havilland practice, and with two Merlin engines predicted performance was so good that it was proposed that no armament need be carried. Despite the radical nature of this proposal a small number were ordered, starting with prototype fighter, bomber and photographic reconnaissance versions. The PR versions were the first in service, closely followed by bomber conversions produced while the initial B.IV production bomber variant was awaited. The latter entered service in May 1942 with No 2 Group, and eventually proved able to carry a bomb load of 4000 lb (1814 kg) – compared with a designed load of 1000 lb (454 kg) – over a range of 1450 miles (2335 km). Performance was up to that envisaged, with a top speed of 380 mph (612 km) enabling the type to carry out unescorted daylight raids.

Meanwhile, No 4 Group in January 1942 was composed of three Halifax, six Whitley and two Wellington squadrons among its operational squadrons. No 5 Group at this time was equipped mainly with Hampdens, which were used by seven of its operational and one reserve squadrons, while one had received Lancasters and three were still using Manchesters.

During 1941 the emphasis in the bombing offensive had changed. At the beginning of the year oil plants were still regarded as the primary target, but as it became clear that there was simply no means by which these could be destroyed in precision attacks – most of the time the weather alone made it impossible for the bomber crews to find them – doubts grew about the value of the offensive. In August it was disclosed that only one in four of those crews who claimed to have found their target had done so, and it was still rare for bombs to fall within five miles of the target.

The appointment of Air Marshal Arthur T Harris as Commander-in-Chief, Bomber Command, on 22 February 1942 marked the completion of the swing towards area bombing tactics. Bomber Command's objective had been redefined a few days earlier to make the undermining of civilian morale its principal task; and by this time the first 100 or so bombers had been equipped with a new navigation aid known as Gee. Gee was based on the use of three radio transmitters broadcasting a complex train of pulses which could be deciphered using a special receiver in the aircraft in conjunction with a specially prepared map of Europe to enable the position to be fixed to within about six miles at a range of 400 miles from the transmitter by

measuring the time intervals between the signals.

Gee was first used operationally in March 1942, with the suitably equipped aircraft using flares and incendiary bombs to light the target – Essen – for the main force to follow. Initial results were disappointing, with only one bomb in 20 falling within five miles of the town. An attack the same month on Lübeck proved more satisfactory, largely because it was easier to find, and the next step was to mount raids involving bigger concentrations of bombers than the 234 launched against Lübeck.

The idea of sending a thousand bombers over Germany in a single night was suggested by Harris to his deputy, Air Vice-Marshal Robert Saundby, in May 1942, and although the normal front-line strength of Bomber Command at this point was no more than 400 aircraft, it was calculated that by using all available bombers, including those currently used by Coastal Command and training units, and by bringing all unserviceable machines up to operational condition, it might just be possible to assemble the magic number. In the event the use of Coastal Command aircraft was vetoed by the Admiralty, which had operational control of the command, but a final total of 940 were finally prepared for the raid.

Above: Mosquitos proved able to carry out unescorted raids and were used for photographic reconnaissance and by the Pathfinder Force. The B.IV was the first bomber variant

Originally scheduled for the night of 27/28 May, the massive raid had to be postponed for three days because of the weather, but in the interval more aircraft became available, so that on the night of 30 May a total of 1046 bombers took off to bomb Cologne. Some 910 of the bombers reached the target, and 39 failed to return; 600 acres of the old city were destroyed, 45,000 people rendered homeless and 469 killed out of a total of around 5000 casualties.

The main result of the raid, however, was to win support for a continued and expanded campaign of area bombing. At that point there was little prospect of attacking Germany in any other way, and with more and bigger bombers Harris was predicting the imminent conclusion of the war as despair spread through Germany. Nothing of the sort was to happen, of course, but more and bigger bombers were what Bomber Command got. Between February 1942 and March 1943 the number of operational aircraft with the command increased from around 500 to over 1000.

At the same time, the techniques employed were becoming more sophisticated. By November 1942 jamming equipment known as Mandrel was being used to jam German Freya early warning radar, and another system code-named Tinsel had been intro- duced to jam radio communications between German night fighters and their ground controllers. These devices were fitted to two bombers in each squadron, and used to screen the others. Another countermeasure introduced alongside Mandrel and Tinsel in July 1943 was Window, which consisted of quantities of aluminium foil strips dropped by the bombers to confuse the Würzburg tracking radar operators by producing hosts of bogus echoes.

The electronic war continued to the end of the war, as new developments in the German detection equipment provoked new countermeasures. In the mean- time, improving the bombers' navigational accuracy was just as vital as protecting them from the German night fighters. In this respect the system known as H2S was a great improvement, being self-contained within the aircraft and providing the operator on board with a representation of the terrain below. At the same time, another system of ground control named Oboe became available. Oboe used a pair of ground transmitters generating signals which were amplified and returned by a transponder on the air- craft, allowing the ground controllers to obtain an exact fix on its positions and control its approach to the target by radio instructions.

The use of Oboe was limited to controlling one aircraft at a time, and its maximum range was about 270 miles (434 km) with the aircraft flying at 28,000 ft (8534 m) because directional signals were used and range was limited by the curvature of the earth. Consequently, the Pathfinder Force, otherwise No 8 Group, Bomber Command, was formed in August 1942 to use the radar aids to illuminate the target with incendiaries. This finally allowed targets in the Ruhr, previously shielded by an all but impenetrable haze of smog, to be located with some accuracy.

For a year, starting in March 1943, Bomber Command carried out a concerted campaign, starting with the Ruhr, switching to Hamburg in July and turning towards Berlin itself in November. Spring brought a change of emphasis during the preliminaries to the Allied landings in Normandy. Thereafter, as the German defences crumbled, the might of Bomber Command was directed against German towns and cities, culminating in the notorious raid on Dresden, when a night raid by more than 800 RAF bombers was followed during the day by 400 USAAF bombers, resulting in the complete destruction of 1600 acres of the city and the death of many thousands of its inhabitants and the refugees who were there.

By the end of the war in Europe, when Bomber Command had reached a strength of 84 operational squadrons, it was equipped with over 2000 aircraft, including 1282 Lancasters, 475 Halifaxes and 265 Mosquitos. In addition, 13 Bomber Support squadrons in No 100 Group disposed of another 260 aircraft, including small numbers of Fortress and Liberator types received from the United States. The latter were only two of the American types used by Bomber Command; others included the Mitchell and Ventura, and all found more extensive employment with other arms of the RAF.

There had also been a number of developments of the basic heavy bombers for special purposes. Among the best known of these were the 'Dambuster' Lancasters equipped with the Barnes Wallis bouncing bombs to attack the Möhne and Eder dams. Lancasters were also the vehicle for the delivery of the biggest conventional (as opposed to nuclear) bombs of the war. These were the 10-ton (10,160 kg) Grand Slams, also developed by Barnes Wallis, and first used against the Bielefeld viaduct in March 1945.

The Tallboy bombs which preceded the Grand Slams were comparative lightweights at 12,000 lb (5443 kg). These were completely different from the earlier bombs of that weight, which were simply 4000-lb (1814-kg) bombs bolted together in threes: the essence of the Tallboy was that it was designed to penetrate deep into the surface after reaching supersonic speeds. The Tallboys proved particularly useful against otherwise impenetrable targets. First used against the Saumur railway tunnel in June 1944, they scored subsequent successes against U-Boat pens and,

perhaps most spectacularly, against the battleship *Tirpitz* in its Norwegian anchorage the following November. A total of 854 Tallboys and 41 Grand Slams were delivered before the end of the war in Europe, adding further laurels to the career of the Lancaster, the only bomber of the time capable of both accommodating and lifting the giant weapons.

Another aspect of the bomber offensive was the provision of the fighter escorts in the later stages of the war. At the start of the bombing offensive no RAF fighter had the necessary range to accompany the bombers on their raids, which was one of the main reasons why they were forced to switch to night attacks. At first this provided protection, but the later generations of German night fighters, equipped with such devices as Naxos, which allowed them to home in on the H2S mapping radar, and Flensburg, which added a new dimension to the electronic war by fixing the bombers' Monica tail warning radar designed to alert the crews that a fighter was on their tail, necessitated a continuing counter-effort. One result was the use of Mosquito night fighters of No 100 Group as specialised electronic support aircraft. One device which these used was known as Perfectos, and used the German fighters' own identification radars, fitted to enable the ground controllers to differentiate between friendly and hostile aircraft, to guide the pilot to an interception. The simple counter to Perfectos was for the German pilots to switch off their identification

equipment, but this had the drawback of making the controllers' task infinitely more difficult.

Fortresses, Stirlings and Halifaxes were equipped with ever more extensive jamming equipment. Biggest of all was Jostle, which jammed the entire frequency range of the German control transmissions. Piperack was another jamming device carried by the bigger bomber support aircraft, and was designed to jam the night fighters' radar rather than its communications.

The overall success of the bombing offensive has been a source of controversy ever since it ended in 1945. Its effects on war production have been debated endlessly, with the conclusion drawn depending on the interpretation of the figures: that production increased throughout the war is indisputable, but what it would have been without the interference of Bomber Command can only be a matter for conjecture. Again, defence against the bombers certainly diverted a good deal of the German war effort from other areas, but only at the cost of 67,000 air crew killed and 4200 wounded on operational service and at the expense of an estimated seven per cent of the British national war effort. What it did prove, not for the first time, was that aerial bombardment strengthens the resolve of the civilian population rather than destroying its morale. Perhaps the most lasting testimony to its validity is in the fantastic cost of rebuilding Europe afterwards, and in the historic cities such as Dresden which were lost to future generations forever.

Left: One of a batch of 20 Boeing B-17Cs supplied to the RAF in 1941 and used briefly by No 91 Squadron. The B-17 was named the Fortress in RAF service

Above: A North American Mitchell of No 28 Squadron, one of the medium bomber squadrons of No 2 Group, returns from a daylight raid over northern France

8 TACTICAL SUPPORT

Following the collapse of Allied resistance in France in May 1940 there was little need for army co-operation work in Europe. The Lysander squadrons that had crossed the Channel to support the BEF were switched to coastal patrol duties on their return, and in December a new Army Co-operation Command was formed. It was in North Africa, however, where the army launched its first offensive of the war in the same month, that the new methods of tactical support were to be developed.

The Mediterranean theatre was something of a backwater until the Italians joined the war in June 1940. During the next year the Italian forces in East Africa were driven out, and Iraq and Syria were secured. The Italians were also driven out of Cyrenaica (eastern Libya) between December 1940 and February 1941, but the arrival of Rommel in North Africa during the latter month presaged a new phase of the war in the desert. While Axis forces blitzkrieged their way through the Balkans and Greece (Crete fell in May), the island of Malta, of vital strategic importance because of its position in the middle of the sea lane between Sicily and the North African coast, came under siege, and Rommel pushed the British and Commonwealth forces back to the frontier of Egypt.

It was only in the summer of 1941 that the obsolescent aircraft that had formed the Middle East Command's strength at the start of the war began to be replaced, and even then much of the new equipment consisted of American aircraft supplied under Lend-Lease. Another problem was one of organisation. Middle East Command at the beginning of 1941 covered a vast area, stretching from British East Africa to the Balkans and from Libya to Iraq, and not only its own organisation but also its communications with the forces on the ground were in need of thorough overhaul.

Following the consolidation of the position in East Africa and Iraq and Syria, and the withdrawal from Greece, this was carried out in the second half of 1941. East Africa was left to South African units, and No 8 Squadron in Aden continued to use Blenheims and Vincents for antisubmarine patrols and internal security duties. Palestine and Transjordan were patrolled by two squadrons of Hurricanes plus a Fleet Air Arm squadron with Albacore fighters and Swordfish torpedo bombers, in addition to a Free French Morane-Saulnier 406 fighter squadron and another Free French flight of Blenheims. Three squadrons, one each of Audaxes, Hurricanes and Vincents, were based in Iraq, and Malta was the base for three squadrons each of Blenheims and Hurricanes, another of Martin Marylands, part of a Wellington squadron and further Fleet Air Arm units.

Air Headquarters, Egypt, included two transport squadrons equipped with Bristol Bombays and Douglas DC-2s plus a General Reconnaissance Unit with Wellingtons, another squadron acting as an Operational Training Unit for Maryland crews and Hurricane squadrons for air defence. No 205 Group in the Suez Canal zone had five long-range bomber squadrons with Wellingtons, and No 201 Group based at Alexandria was equipped with a variety of types for air-sea rescue and reconnaissance.

At the same time, in November 1941, the forward units acting in support of the ground forces were reconstituted as Air Headquarters, Western Desert. In addition to the HQ squadrons with a variety of transport, reconnaissance, fighter and light bomber types, there were three fighter and two light bomber wings, the former with Hurricanes and Tomahawks and the latter using Blenheims and Marylands. An important aspect of these wings was that they were intended to be fully mobile, but while the necessary transport vehicles were awaited a new system of co-operation with the ground forces was evolved.

Above: A Martin Baltimore lands at Accra after crossing the Atlantic on its way to join the RAF in the North African desert

Previous page: A pair of Spitfire Vs over the Allied beachhead at Anzio

It had been recognised by this stage that the first requirement for effective air support was local air superiority, and the fighters were able to achieve this under RAF control. Support of the ground forces was a more complicated matter however: since the desert war was one of rapid movement, it was often difficult for the air controllers to know the precise location of the Allied lines. To overcome this problem, a new system of Air Support Controls was established to co-ordinate requests for air support and relay these to the airfields, to the aircraft in the air and to the Air Headquarters. At the same time, air-ground co-ordination was improved by new rules for indicating targets and establishing bomb lines ahead of the Allied troops. Finally, to back up the front-line units, the maintenance situation was improved by the establishment of a new system for the retrieval and repair of damaged aircraft, the supply of aircraft and spares and the storage of supplies.

Consequently, the air forces were able to intensify their efforts against the Luftwaffe. At night the Wellingtons attacked the German airfields and the supply convoys crossing the Mediterranean, and during the day the light bombers struck at the forward air bases. The see-saw battles that continued until the turning point at Alamein in August 1942 were accompanied by a steady improvement in both the quantity and the quality of the air support, and the development of specialised ground-attack aircraft.

Early equipment of the squadrons in North Africa had included a number of American designs. Several of the South African Air Force squadrons were equipped with Curtiss Mohawks and Tomahawks, the latter also being used by RAF and Royal Australian Air Force units. These corresponded to the USAAC's P-36 and P-40, the latter being an improved version with an Allison V-1710 in-line engine in place of the earlier model's Double Wasp or Cyclone radial. Original armament was six machine guns, but as later models, named Kittyhawk in RAF service, became available the standard armament was reduced to four wing-mounted 0.5-in Brownings plus a 500-lb (227-kg) bomb under the fuselage or smaller bombs under the wings.

A number of American light bomber types were also used by the RAF in the desert war. The Martin Maryland, like the Douglas Boston, was originally ordered by France, and along with other aircraft in production for the French after May 1940 was taken over by the RAF. The Martin Baltimore was a redesigned Maryland built to RAF specifications, and after early models were delivered with manually aimed Vickers K guns in the dorsal position a Boulton Paul powered turret was installed in the Mk III and a Martin turret in the Mk IV. For close-support work the Baltimore also had a battery of ventral machine guns; two Vickers K guns were standard but some had four or six guns firing downward to the rear as well as four wing-mounted guns, and the bombload of 2000 lb (907 kg) remained the same as that of the Maryland.

Martin Maryland attack bombers
serving with the Desert Air Force

The original armament of the Hurricane was also increased for the ground-attack role, and after the Mk IIB had introduced 12.303-in Brownings, the Mk IIC was fitted with four 20-mm Hispano cannon, both versions being equipped to carry a 250-lb (113-kg) bomb under each wing. A more specialised variant was the Mk IID, which carried a 40-mm cannon under each wing specifically to attack tanks, and later examples designated Mk IV and V were fitted with wings that could carry cannon, bombs, drop tanks or four 60-lb (27-kg) rockets each.

Meanwhile, the siege of Malta was intensified. In the first four months of 1942 some 10,000 tons (10,160,000 kg) of bombs had been dropped on the island, before early May brought the arrival of Spitfire reinforcements and the withdrawal of the bulk of the German bomber force from Sicily. However, while the assault lasted the Axis convoys were able to reach Tripoli, and in June Rommel began a new advance.

At this point the front was still west of Gazala, where it had stabilised at the end of Operation Crusader in February. In May the fighting was renewed and, after turning the Allied line, Rommel was able to drive forward, pushing back the Eighth Army 400 miles (644 km) in two weeks. A remarkable feature of this retreat was the preservation of the fighting force relatively intact, which in the case of the RAF squadrons was a result of the preparation of landing grounds at intervals all the way back to the frontier. The squadrons were divided into two parts, leapfrogging backwards over each other, cleaning out the supplies as they went and not leaving each base until the enemy was within 20 miles (32 km) or so – a distance judged approximately by the sight of their own bombs bursting. At the same time, the advancing German forces were kept under constant air bombardment.

By the beginning of July the advance had been halted at the defensive line at Alamein, while the aircraft kept up their attacks. The Baltimore and Boston light bombers had by now displaced the heavy Wellingtons from the Canal Zone: the former, escorted by Kittyhawks, carried out daylight attacks while Spitfires maintained air superiority and the Hurricane fighter bombers sought out their own targets, and at night the Wellingtons attacked Tobruk, now a German base, from their new bases in Palestine, refuelling in the Canal Zone en route.

In June and July the Wellingtons were joined in Palestine by Nos 159 and 160 Squadrons, on their way to India with Liberator B.IIs. Coastal Command had earlier equipped several squadrons with Liberators, and the B.II was the first bomber version to serve with the RAF. Powered by four Twin Wasp radials and armed with quadruple 0.303-in Brownings in Boulton Paul tail and dorsal turrets, plus single hand-aimed weapons of the same calibre in the nose and on each side of the waist, the Liberator B.II could carry 5000 lb (2268 kg) of bombs over a range of 2100 miles (3379 km). They were thus able to attack the principal Axis supply port of Benghazi, in Libya, previously a regular target for the Wellingtons, direct from their base in Palestine, and were retained in Palestine until the autumn for that purpose.

Between the consolidation of the Alamein line in July and the Allied Operation Torch landings in Morocco and Algeria in November, the various groups of RAF Middle East helped to seal the fate of the Afrika Korps, preventing supplies reaching the German and Italian armies, making concerted attacks impossible and maintaining the defence of Malta. During the pursuit of the Axis forces across Libya they kept up the work of harassing the enemy columns.

The desert war was far from over, but Rommel's ultimate defeat was now only a matter of time. In the meantime, the grand strategy for the defeat of the Axis had to be decided, and in January 1943 Churchill and Roosevelt met in Casablanca to work out the immediate objectives. It was decided to invade Sicily, since an invasion across the English Channel was not practicable during the new year.

For the RAF, this meant a new organisation to integrate the strategic bomber, tactical support and coastal formations with the growing American air strength in the Mediterranean theatre. The result was the Mediterranean Air Command, composed of RAF, Commonwealth and USAAF elements and subdivided into a series of subordinate commands. The bulk of the new force was divided between RAF Middle East and the Northwest African Air Forces, but there were also Air Headquarters at Gibraltar and Malta as well as the Mediterranean Air Transport Service, with two USAAF squadrons of Dakotas and No 216 Group, whose seven squadrons, including two South African Air Force units, operated various transport and communications types.

At the start of the invasion of Sicily in July 1943, Air Headquarters, Malta comprised a total of six squadrons of Spitfires, including one of the SAAF, three of Beaufighters and one of Mosquitos, plus a squadron each of Baltimores and Wellingtons. At Gibraltar there were two squadrons each of Hudsons and Catalinas, along with another of Wellingtons and detachments of Beaufighters and Spitfires.

Under RAF Middle East Headquarters came three special squadrons, one equipped with Liberators and Halifaxes used to supply resistance fighters in Greece, Albania and Yugoslavia, another using Wellingtons and Blenheims for radar calibration, as well as the

occasional bombing raid, while the third had Spitfires and Hurricanes for photographic reconnaissance. No 201 Group continued in its coastal and maritime reconnaissance role, its four RAF, one Greek, two SAAF, two Royal Australian Air Force and two Fleet Air Arm squadrons using Beaufighters, Baltimores, Blenheims, Wellingtons, Hudsons, Walruses and Swordfishes. The US Ninth Air Force also came under RAF Middle East, its 20 squadrons of Liberators serving alongside one RAF and one RAAF squadrons of Halifaxes, though other units were attached to Northwest African Tactical Air Force and Troop Carrier Command.

Other components of RAF Middle East were Air Headquarters in the Levant, where one squadron of Hurricanes was based; Iraq and Persia, with a squadron of Blenheims and a detachment of Hurricanes; East Africa, which extended as far as South Africa and deployed four squadrons of Catalinas for anti-submarine patrols over the Indian Ocean; and British Forces Aden, where a flight of Catalinas and a squadron of Blenheims were based. Finally, there was Air Defences, Eastern Mediterranean, whose 16 squadrons of Hurricanes included three SAAF and one RAAF, and which also incorporated two squadrons of Beaufighters and one of Spitfires.

Northwest African Air Forces were again composed of various formations devoted to different functions. The biggest of these, Northwest African Tactical Air Force, was further divided between the Desert Air Force, the US XII Air Support Command and the Tactical Bomber Force. Other components of the NWAAF were the Strategic Air Force, Troop Carrier Command, Coastal Air Force and the Photographic Reconnaissance Wing.

RAF, SAAF, RAAF and Royal Canadian Air

The Duke of Gloucester at Ismailia, with a Consolidated Liberator behind him. The long-range Liberator was the principal heavy bomber in the North African campaign

Force units formed the Desert Air Force, which included 17 squadrons of Spitfires, six of Kittyhawks, and one each of Hurricanes and Mosquitos, alongside six USAAF squadrons of Warhawks. The Tactical Bomber Force included eight squadrons of Boston and Baltimore light bombers, of which three were SAAF, plus a squadron each of Spitfires and Hurricanes for tactical reconnaissance. XII Air Support Command, the third component of the Desert Air Force consisted of 16 squadrons of Mustangs, Warhawks (as Kittyhawks were known in American service) and Spitfires.

The Strategic Air Force was primarily an American affair, including 36 squadrons of Flying Fortress, Mitchell and Marauder bombers plus 12 squadrons of Lightning and Warhawk fighters. There were, however, a further six RAF and three RCAF squadrons equipped with Wellingtons. The Coastal Air Force, on the other hand, had a majority of RAF squadrons, which included six of Beaufighters, three of Hurricanes, two each of Blenheims, Wellingtons, Hudsons, Spitfires and Walrus air-sea rescue machines, plus one each of Marauders and Baltimores. The American contribution comprised two squadrons of Liberators, six of Airacobras and three of Spitfires.

The two remaining components of the Northwest African Air Forces, Troop Carrier Command and the Photographic Reconnaissance Wing, were predominantly American. The former had a squadron of RAF Albemarles and a detachment of Halifaxes, but the 27 squadrons of USAAF Dakotas formed its major carrying capacity. The smaller PR Wing included a squadron of Spitfires and detachments of Mosquitos,

along with two squadrons of Lightnings and one of Flying Fortresses.

Following the successful invasion of Sicily and the subsequent landings in Italy itself, and then the long struggle to defeat the German armies after the armistice with Italy in September 1943, there was a rationalisation of these various commands. The subordinate formations under Middle East Command continued to be based on their geographical locations, but the Northwest African Air Forces merged with Mediterranean Air Command. The result was a similar division of responsibilities, but the various arms now consisted of the Mediterranean Allied Tactical, Strategic and Coastal Air Forces, the Desert Air Force continuing to form the major part of the tactical air force.

At the same time, June 1944 brought the formation of a new command, the Balkan Air Force, which was established to assist the growing resistance movement in occupied Greece and, particularly, Yugoslavia. The equipment of the new arm, a representative selection of the various types equipping the main forces in the theatre, enabled it to carry out similar tasks: bombing attacks on supply and communications facilities, anti-shipping strikes, the disruption of German landings on the Adriatic islands, the dropping and landing of arms and other supplies to the resistance forces and fighter-bomber attacks on targets of opportunity such as troop trains. A particularly notable achievement of the Balkan Air Force was the large-scale evacuation of wounded partisans, some 11,000 of whom were flown out from improvised airstrips to hospitals in Italy. In addition, another 2500 people were landed in occupied territory, and a total of 16,400 tons (16,662,400 kg) of supplies were delivered.

At the same time as preparations were under way in the Mediterranean for the invasion of Sicily and Italy, the longer-range planning for the inevitable cross-Channel invasion was also under way in Britain. Almost as soon as the German daylight bombing raids had ceased in the autumn of 1940, Fighter Command had begun a programme of raids over the continent. Among the operations carried out were those code-named Circus, involving heavily escorted groups of light bombers whose real purpose was to provoke a response from the German fighter defences. A handful of Blenheims might be accompanied by 20 or more squadrons of fighters, but just as the Hurricanes had been outclassed by improved models of the Bf 109, so that they were used first for low-level escort of the bombers, and then more and more as fighter-bombers, so the Spitfires began to meet superior opposition in the form of the Focke-Wulf Fw 190.

As a result, heavy losses began to be suffered both from the sparse but effective fighter opposition and from the fierce anti-aircraft fire that was normally encountered around any important target. The same applied to the Roadstead anti-shipping strikes that were another regular feature of Fighter Command

operations in 1941, and while the Rhubarb strikes (carried out by one or two fighters at low level) generally managed to evade interception they were more useful as training exercises for the pilots than for the damage caused.

At the same time, the German tactics had changed to include similar operations, and a degree of specialisation in fighter design was obviously called for. The Spitfire V that had been introduced in March 1941 with 1440-hp Merlin 45 or 50 engines was fitted with A, B or C wings able to carry alternative armament of eight .303-in Brownings, four Brownings and two 20-mm cannon, or four cannon. The Mk VB was the standard fighter version in 1941–42, and while the specialised Mk VII high-altitude version and Mk VIII all-purpose version were under development the Mk VI, with a pressurised cabin, was produced as an interim measure. At the same time, the necessity to combat the Fw 190 led to the installation of the more powerful 60-series Merlin engine in a basic Mk V airframe.

The resulting Spitfire IX was ultimately built in greater numbers than any other variant except the Mk V, and to equip it for different roles it was given extended wingtips for enhanced high-altitude performance, or clipped wings for fast low-level flight. Similar modifications were made to produce low-

A Martin Marauder, another of the medium bombers to serve with the Allied air forces in the North African and Mediterranean theatres

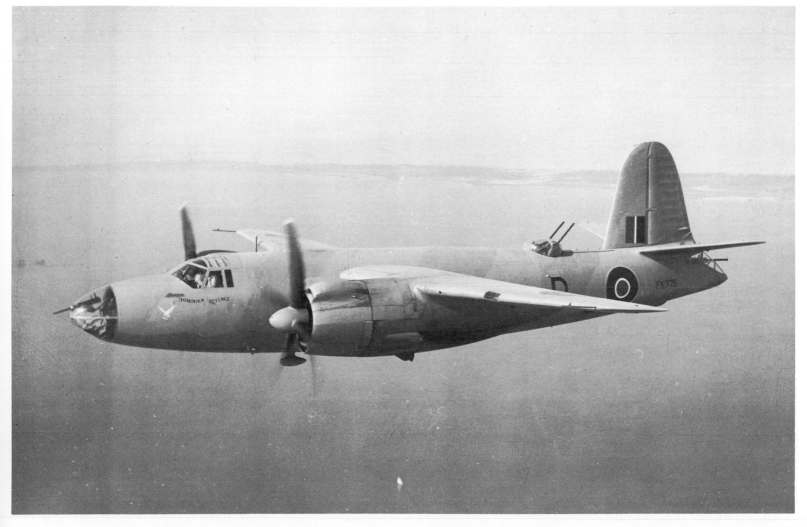

altitude Mk Vs, but by this time an even better low-level fighter had appeared in the form of the Hawker Typhoon. In fact, it was some time before the Typhoon's abilities in this role were recognised, and trouble with the powerplant, the Napier Sabre, delayed its acceptance, while poor altitude performance almost caused its withdrawal from service. By 1942, however, it had demonstrated its ability to catch low-flying Fw 190s which had taken to low-level sweeps on Rhubarb lines. The Typhoon was also used along with the twin-engined Westland Whirlwind for attacks on Channel shipping, but while the Whirlwind only equipped two squadrons and was replaced by 1943, the Typhoon went on to become a highly successful ground-attack fighter, carrying 1000-lb (454-kg) bombs or eight 3-in rockets as well as its normal armament of four 20-mm cannon.

Another new fighter of 1941 which excelled at low altitudes was the North American Mustang, originally ordered in 1940 by the purchasing mission to the United States. The original Mustang I was used by 14 squadrons of Army Co-operation Command, but later models, which replaced the Mk I's Allison engine with a Packard-built Merlin showed a dramatic improvement in performance at all levels, and shone particularly as a long-range bomber escort. The Mk Is were used mainly for tactical reconnaissance and Rhubarb sweeps over the continent.

By June 1943 the strength of Fighter Command had reached 102 squadrons, though 20 of these were tactical support units temporarily allocated to the command. The main fighter strength included 43 squadrons of Spitfires, 14 of Typhoons, 10 of Beaufighters, 10 of Mosquitos, two of Whirlwinds and one each of Defiants and Bostons. The army support component included 13 squadrons of Mustangs, one each of Tomahawks and Hurricanes and five of Taylorcraft Auster III Air Observation Post machines. The Austers operated in close co-operation with army units for liaison and artillery observation, flying from any convenient field, and often crewed by army pilots and observers.

In August 1942 Fighter Command fought its biggest single battle of the war in support of the raid on Dieppe. Hurricane fighter-bombers, along with the light bombers of No 2 Group, supported the troops carrying out the landing by laying smoke screens and attacking defensive strongpoints, while the Spitfire squadrons maintained a defensive umbrella overhead. During the day of 19 August 2617 sorties were flown by RAF aircraft, of which 106 were lost. Some high claims were made for the number of Luftwaffe aircraft destroyed, though it was calculated after the war that German losses amounted to only 48, with a further 24 damaged. They were kept away from the landing forces with great success, but at the same time some other lessons were learned. One was the futility of firing aircraft guns against concrete emplacements, another was the need for more comprehensive control of the aircraft.

Accordingly, towards the end of 1943 a new command was formed for the support of the D-Day landings. Named the 2nd Tactical Air Force, the new organisation incorporated the various elements of Army Support Command, the light bombers of No 2 Group, Bomber Command and many of Fighter Command's squadrons. In addition, there were heavy bombers and transports adapted for paratroop dropping and glider towing to transport the airborne forces.

In the months leading up to the invasion, too, there was heated debate about the use of the strategic bomber forces. Bomber Command and US Eighth Air Force commanders wanted to continue undistracted with the strategic offensive which many of them considered would make the landings unnecessary: the men responsible for planning the operation, on the other hand, wanted a concerted offensive against enemy communications which would simultaneously help to convince the defending forces that the invasion would be carried out in the Calais region, help to draw labour away from the construction of defences, and prevent reinforcements reaching the landing area in Normandy.

In the end, the tasks the air forces were called on to carry out were summarised under five headings: maintaining air superiority; continuous reconnaissance of enemy dispositions and movements; the disruption of communications and supply lines;

500-lb (227-kg) bombs about to be loaded on a Hawker Typhoon IB of No 175 Squadron, 2nd Tactical Air Force

A newly built Handley Page Halifax II on a test flight

offensive strikes against enemy naval forces; and air-lift of the airborne forces. For the actual assault phase, the objectives were the protection of the invasion fleets; neutralising the beaches where the troops would land; protecting the beaches after the landings; and disrupting enemy movements and communications during the landings.

To this end, the 2nd TAF disposed of an impressive 96 squadrons, including Commonwealth units, divided between six groups. No 38 Group, with four squadrons of Albemarles, four of Stirlings and two of Halifaxes, along with No 46 Group's five squadrons of Dakotas, were allocated to paratroop dropping and glider towing. No 2 Group of light bombers included two squadrons of Bostons, four of Mitchells and six of Mosquitos. The two fighter-bomber groups, Nos 83 and 84, together comprised 28 squadrons of Spitfires, 18 of Typhoons and 11 of Mustangs. No 85 Group, whose task was air defence of the overseas base, had four squadrons of Spitfires, two of the Tempest development of the Typhoon, and six of Mosquito night fighters. This group operated under the command of No 11 Group, now part of Air Defence of Great Britain and the other component of the Allied Expeditionary Air Force which had been created to control the 2nd TAF, which in turn was responsible to ADGB for night operations and 2nd TAF for day.

During the D-Day landings and the subsequent fighting north towards Germany the two principal tasks of the 2nd TAF resolved themselves into reconnaissance and close support, directing attacks against tanks, troop concentrations and other targets at the request of the ground commanders. Air superiority was the prerequisite for the success of these operations, which were helped by the destruction of bridges and the disruption of transport and communications. The rocket-firing fighters proved particularly useful in destroying trains and armour.

As the Allied armies advanced across Europe, another threat was posed to Air Defence of Great Britain by the new flying bombs. The launching sites had been subject to attacks since late 1943, but new ramps were erected almost as quickly as old ones were destroyed, and after the flying bomb offensive opened on 12 June the number of launches mounted rapidly. Consequently, the fighters of No 11 Group were called on to intercept the V-1s, as they became known. The most successful interceptors of V-1s were the Hawker Tempests, and another new fighter used for the task was the Gloster Meteor, the world's first fully operational jet aircraft, which equipped a single squadron in the summer of 1944.

The pushing back of the German lines eventually ended the flying bomb offensive, as it was no longer possible for them to reach England, but at the same time the V-2 rockets began to be directed against London. There was no hope of intercepting these once they had been launched, and bomb-carrying Spitfires were used to attack their launching sites in Holland instead.

In October 1944 ADGB reverted to its name of Fighter Command, leaving the 2nd TAF to continue its support of the Allied armies' advance towards Berlin. The fighter-bombers extended their activities to include attacks on enemy headquarters buildings, and their success in the tactical support role was vividly illustrated during the German offensive in the Ardennes in December 1944. Between 16 December, when the offensive began, and 23 December the German advance averaged 12 miles a day. During that week, however, the weather had prevented operational flying: on 24 December, when the weather lifted sufficiently to allow nearly 600 sorties to be flown, the advance was slowed dramatically, and by the following day it had come to a halt.

Left: Pilot and liaison officer with an Auster Aerial Observation Post aircraft

Below: Bostons of the 2nd Tactical Air Force prepare for take-off

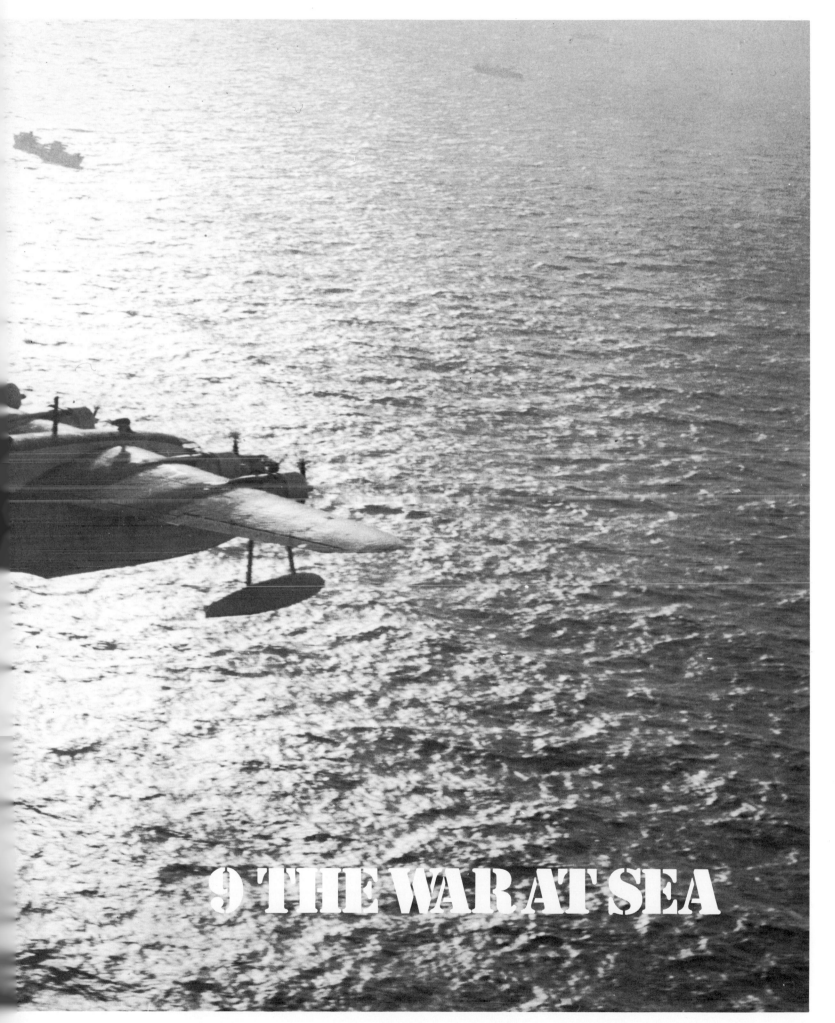

9 THE WAR AT SEA

During the Second World War, as in the First, one of Germany's most dangerous offensives was directed against the shipping on which Britain's war effort depended. When war was declared German U-Boats, pocket battleships and commerce raiders were already at sea, and within hours the *U-30* had sunk the liner *Athenia* 200 miles (322 km) west of the Hebrides. This was a mistake: the U-Boats were under orders to attack military targets only, and *U 30's* commander had mistaken the liner for a troop ship. Nevertheless, it was an early reminder of the dangers to Britain's supply lines, and it hastened the introduction of convoys.

Unfortunately, there were few ships available to escort the convoys, and they were of limited endurance, so that at first the convoys could only be escorted for the first 300 miles (483 km) of the west-bound journey, after which they dispersed to make their own way. Incoming convoys normally had an armed merchant cruiser as escort as far as the 300-mile (483-km) limit, with a naval escort joining them at that point.

It had been found during the First World War that aircraft, with their extended view, were a great deterrent to submarines in the vicinity of convoys, but the problem in 1939 was the lack of long-range patrol aircraft. The Fleet Air Arm had been completely separated from the RAF shortly before the outbreak of war, but there were too few carriers to accompany the convoys. Also the land-based aircraft of Coastal Command were limited to a radius of about 500 miles (800 km) from the coast. For the U-Boat threat to be contained, there were many requirements, starting with longer-range aircraft, but also including a more efficient patrol system and, most important of all in the long run, effective methods of locating and attacking submarines.

By 1939 there were three new types on order for Coastal Command. One of these was the Blackburn Botha, designed to a 1935 specification and ordered off the drawing board in 1936. Unfortunately, the Botha's entry into service in the summer of 1940 revealed it to be both underpowered and otherwise unsuitable for the task, and it was used only briefly for patrols over the North Sea before being relegated to training. Another failure was the Saunders-Roe Lerwick, a twin-engined flying boat which proved unstable in the air and was cancelled after only 21 had been built.

Fortunately, the third of the new types was a success. The Bristol Beaufort avoided the problems of the Botha by replacing the specified Bristol Perseus engines with the more powerful Taurus. Between November 1939 and June 1940 Beauforts replaced the two squadrons of Vildebeests, previously Coastal Command's only torpedo bombers, and equipped one new squadron as well as replacing Ansons in two others. The type also served with two squadrons in the Mediterranean, but its true potential was reached with the redesigned Beaufighter.

The Beaufighter combined the wings and tail of the Beaufort with a new, slimmer fuselage housing a two-man crew instead of the original four, and Bristol Hercules engines. Early Beaufighters achieved great success as radar-equipped night fighters, and with the 1595-hp Hercules XVI engines the Mk IVC succeeded the Mk Ic in 1942. The Mk IVC added a torpedo-carrying capability to the 1500-mile (2415-km) range of the earlier version, and provided a useful extension of Coastal Command's patrol range.

The early stages of the U-Boat campaign were actually reasonably well contained: the convoy routes were switched away from the southwestern approach to the English Channel to the northwest. By the end of March 1940, when the U-Boats were recalled for the Norwegian invasion, 199 merchant ships had been sunk, but so had 18 U-Boats, and the British naval blockade was proving successful in preventing supplies reaching Germany.

However, the occupation of Norway in April and then of France in May and June changed the situation dramatically in Germany's favour. Now long-range

Left: A Bristol Beaufort II based on Malta for strikes against Axis shipping in the Mediterranean

Below: The Saunders-Roe Lerwick was intended for large-scale service with Coastal Command, but proved unstable and production was abandoned at an early stage

Focke-Wulf Fw 200 Condor aircraft could use bases in Norway to attack shipping in the northern waters, and the U-Boats were provided with new bases in the Bay of Biscay, allowing them much easier access to the mid-Atlantic. During the second half of 1940 losses of merchant shipping reached an average of 450,000 tons (457,200,000 kg) a month, nearly 60 per cent of which was sunk by U-Boats, while the Condors sank 12 per cent and mines and surface ships were responsible for the remainder.

At this point there was a suggestion that Coastal Command should follow the Fleet Air Arm in becoming part of the Royal Navy, but neither service was in favour of this, and the solution was found in the creation of combined headquarters, with the command remaining part of the RAF but being placed under the operational control of the Admiralty from April 1941. No 15 Group headquarters were located at Liverpool alongside the new Western Naval Command, and a new group, No 19, was formed at Plymouth to co-operate with the naval command there.

Early in 1941 a squadron of Hudsons and another of Sunderlands were based in Iceland to extend the patrol area in the mid-Atlantic, and a similar force was based in Liberia to patrol the sealanes off western Africa. Nevertheless, the rate of sinkings was already exceeding the rate of replacement, and during the first few months of 1941 it rose again, reaching a total of 644,000 tons (654,304,000 kg) in April, with nearly half of the total being accounted for by aircraft.

At the same time, there were some encouraging developments. On 6 April a suicidal attack by a Beaufort of No 22 Squadron succeeded in severely damaging the battle-cruiser *Gneisenau* in the harbour at Brest. Towards the end of May a Catalina flying boat of No 209 Squadron succeeded in locating the battleship *Bismarck* in the mid-Atlantic, and the ensuing air and sea operations resulted in the sinking of another serious threat. Equally significant was the loss to the German Navy in March of three of the most experienced U-Boat commanders.

Evasive routing of the convoys and the gradual extension of air patrols and escort protection for convoys, coupled with the sinking or containment of the principal German surface ships resulted in a dramatic reduction in the number of merchant vessels sunk in June and July. This was partly a result of the strengthening of No 15 Group's Atlantic patrols in the western approaches, following the introduction of Bomber Command Blenheims on North Sea patrol duties, while the use of catapult-armed merchantmen, carrying a single Hurricane which could be launched to fight off the Condors whose reconnaissance was vital to the success of the U-Boats also helped. After an increase in the figures for August and September, the remainder of the year saw dramatic falls in losses in the

Atlantic, though this was mainly a result of the U-Boats being switched to operations in the Mediterranean.

The new year, with the entry of the United States into the war, brought an alarming increase in losses. Convoys were not immediately adopted by the Americans, and U-Boats operating off the northeastern coast of the United States were able to sink 505 ships in the area before the introduction of convoys at the end of June. The U-Boats then changed their area of operations again, to the 'black gaps' in the mid-Atlantic, where no air cover could be provided. Throughout 1942 Allied losses averaged 650,000 tons (660, 400,000 kg) per month, still short of the 800,000 tons (812,800,000 kg) the Germans considered necessary to achieve a decisive victory, but also well ahead of the rate of replacement. Moreover, US commitments in the Pacific, the demands for convoys to the northern Russian ports, and the requirements of the convoys for the Torch landings in North Africa were combining to stretch the escort forces still further.

Consequently, the beginning of 1943 marked the crucial stage in the battle for the Atlantic sealanes. The U-Boat commanders had many months of experience behind them, and with the benefit of intelligence provided by the cryptanalysts, who had succeeded in breaking the convoy cypher, they were able to mount a concerted attack on the March convoys. In that month 39 U-Boats intercepted two convoys bound for Britain, sinking a total of 21 ships. This success marked the high point in the battle as far as Germany was concerned. In the following months a combination of new aircraft and equipment was to turn the battle decisively in the Allies' favour.

One of the most important innovations was the

development of centimetric ASV (air-to-surface-vessel) radar, which enabled aircraft fitted with the equipment to locate surfaced submarines at night. The first ASV Mk III radar sets, converted from H2S equipment intended for bombers but diverted to Coastal Command when it was realised that the U-Boats were equipped with receivers that could detect the emissions of the earlier, and less useful, radar transmitters, were installed in Liberators towards the end of 1942.

Another development, designed to improve the efficiency of the earlier ASV sets, was giving the patrol aircraft a means of illuminating U-Boats which had been detected. Within about three-quarters of a mile (one and a fifth km) of the target the U-Boat became indistinguishable from the general reflections from the sea surface. The answer came in the fairly obvious form of a powerful searchlight – named the Leigh Light after its inventor – which could be switched on to light up the submarine once the radar set had tracked it to the limit of its detection range. The first installa-

tions were tried as early as January 1941, but its service introduction was delayed as a result of the unfortunate Turbinlite programme for night fighters. The latter was given priority, although its diffused beam was quite different from the concentrated beam of the Leigh Light, and it was only after the Turbinlite's unsuitability had been demonstrated that full-scale trials of the Leigh Light were carried out.

These were made by Wellingtons of No 172 Squadron in June 1942 in the Bay of Biscay, and proved resoundingly successful. The result was that the U-Boats were forced to travel submerged through the Bay of Biscay on their way to and from their bases, severely limiting the amount of time they could spend on active patrol in the Atlantic.

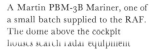

A Martin PBM-3B Mariner, one of a small batch supplied to the RAF. The dome above the cockpit houses search radar equipment

Having detected a submarine using radar or Leigh Light, an aircraft then needed an effective weapon with which to attack it. The use of bombs against submarines had quickly proved unproductive, and the standard Mk VII depth charge was not much better. By 1942 the Mk VIII depth charge had been introduced: filled with Torpex instead of the less powerful Amatol and with a pistol that could be set to detonate it at a depth of 25 ft (7.6 m) this proved much more effective.

Finally, the provision of Very Long Range Liberators early in 1943 enabled the gaps in the Atlantic patrols to be filled, and immediately the rate of Allied losses began to decline, while the sinkings of U-Boats showed a dramatic increase. Two months after the March convoys had been intercepted with such success, another convoy battle took place in the Atlantic. This time, however, with more escorts available and aircraft using the new radar, the U-Boats were on the receiving end and eight of the 12 attacking submarines were sunk.

Within the next three months the U-Boat battle was all but over. The waters of the Bay of Biscay became so dangerous that the submarines themselves were forced to travel in convoys with air escorts, but combined operations by aircraft and naval forces caused the abandonment of this tactic too. The introduction of snorkels to allow the U-Boats to recharge their batteries without surfacing reduced the chances of detection, but at the cost of inhibiting their freedom of movement. Acoustic torpedoes introduced at the beginning of 1943 were soon countered by escorts towing noise making devices behind them to decoy the homing mechanism. The revolutionary new Walther propulsion system, using hydrogen peroxide fuel in a closed cycle steam turbine to free the vessel of the need for constant recharging of batteries, raised as many problems as it solved.

By this stage, in any case, Germany no longer had the capacity to man enough submarines. The demands of the war effort were such that the new boats being built at the rate of 25–30 per month in 1943 could only be crewed by transferring officers from the army and air force. The U-Boats continued to be dangerous, switching tactics and changing their areas of operation repeatedly, but the strength of the naval escorts was steadily increased by the provision of merchant ships converted into temporary aircraft carriers, and in conjunction with the land-based patrol aircraft and the Sunderland and Catalina flying boats they kept the U-Boats on the defensive for the remainder of the war.

The battle against the U-Boats was not Coastal Command's only responsibility during the war. From June 1941 the Photographic Reconnaissance Unit, using Spitfires and Mosquitos equipped with high-resolution cameras in heated installations to prevent them freezing up, had been part of Coastal Command, and by October 1942 there were five squadrons employed on this work. Their tasks included photographing targets after bombing raids to assess damage, searching out radar transmitters, providing detailed pictures of the landing sites in the preliminary planning of the Allied invasions, monitoring shipping movements in German-controlled ports and, following the invasion of France, providing detailed pictures of enemy positions that were about to be attacked.

Another vital aspect of Coastal Command operations was the air-sea rescue service of aircrew in home waters. The peak year for this activity was 1943, when 1648 individuals were retrieved, 708 of them in the third quarter. Regular meteorological flights were made to chart conditions in the upper atmosphere and over the North Sea and Atlantic, gaining information of the highest importance in planning air raids and, most notably, the D-Day landings.

A Short Sunderland I, original version of one of the mainstays of Coastal Command's battle against the U-Boats

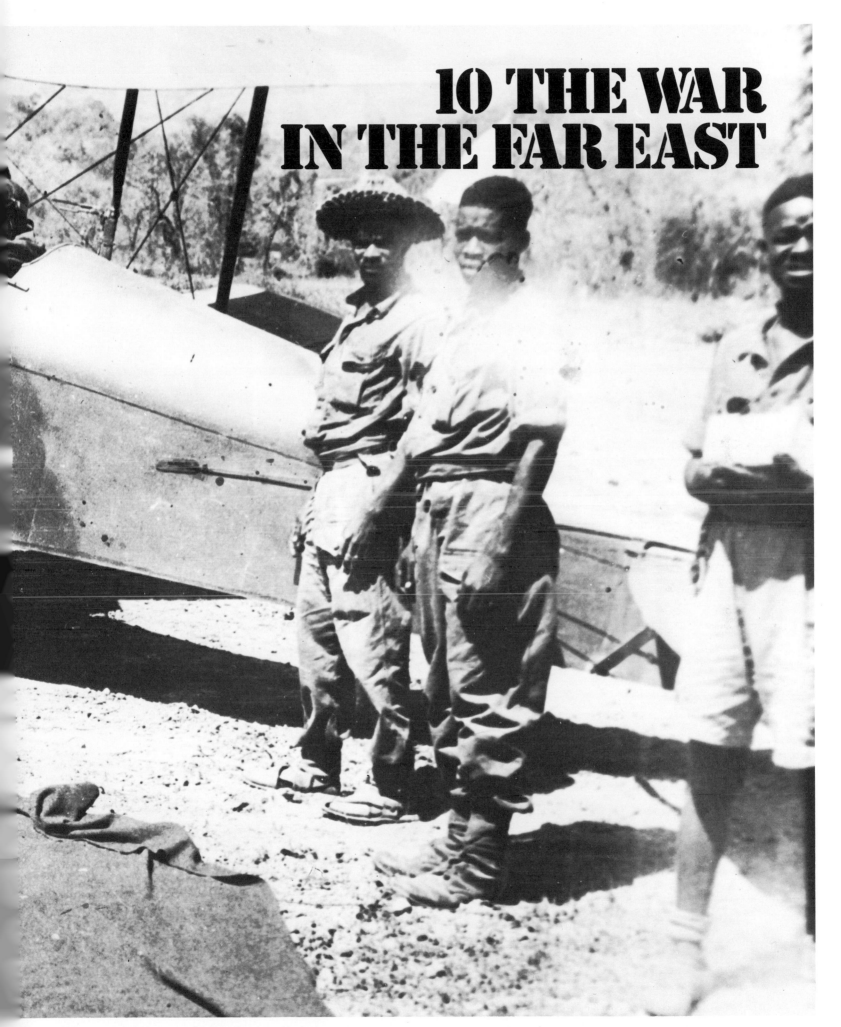

At the start of the war in Europe the island of Singapore, Britain's main naval base in the Far East, was defended by a battery of 15-in guns and a few squadrons of obsolete aircraft. Trenchard's suggestion 15 years earlier that the RAF should provide the main defence of the island had been rejected, and the guns were installed because it was anticipated that Singapore would be attacked from the sea. During 1940, however, it was realised that the Royal Navy was not in a position to do much about the island's defence, and the RAF was given responsibility for protecting it against a possible Japanese invasion.

Unfortunately, by this stage the RAF was itself overstretched. In October 1940 it was estimated that 566 aircraft was the minimum first-line strength required to defend the British interests in the Far East: by the beginning of December 1941 the total had reached 362, of which 233 were serviceable, and almost all of which were thoroughly outmoded. In Singapore itself there were four squadrons of Blen-

heims and two of Vildebeests. The Sunderland squadron had been transferred, first to Ceylon and then to Egypt, and in its place there was a single squadron of Catalina flying boats. The Royal Australian Air Force provided two squadrons of Hudsons and two of Brewster Buffalos: the latter, ordered from the United States in 1939, had been rejected for service in Europe, and was shipped out to the Far East, where it was thought at least capable of dealing with Japanese opposition. One RAF and one RNZAF squadron were also equipped with Buffalos by December 1941.

Elsewhere in the Far East the situation was hardly any better. Ceylon (Sri Lanka) was still defended by a single squadron equipped with a mixture of Vildebeests and Seal floatplanes. In Burma there was another squadron of Buffalos and a few Blenheims of No 60 Squadron, most of whose aircraft were at Singapore. Hong Kong and Borneo had no air defences. However the Japanese, widely believed to have no worth-while combat aircraft, had been at war with

Previous page: A wounded East African soldier waits for evacuation by air during the retreat from Burma

China since 1937 and actually had some extremely capable combat machines, including the Zero, one of the best fighters in the world at that time.

Under orders to refrain from provoking Japanese aggression, the squadrons at Singapore could do little. Hudsons spotted Japanese convoys 300 miles (483 km) off the coast of the Malayan peninsula on 29 November 1941, but contact was lost when the weather impeded further reconnaissance flights. By the time the news of the attack on Pearl Harbor reached Singapore the Japanese landings had already begun.

During the following weeks British resistance was crushed. Six squadrons had been deployed in the Malayan peninsula, but most of their aircraft were destroyed on the ground. The remainder could do little to halt the air raids on Singapore itself, and by the end of January 1942 most of the surviving aircraft had been withdrawn to Sumatra, where the story was repeated, and the final remnants continued the fight on Java, until there were simply no more aircraft left

to fly. In Burma, the Blenheims of No 60 Squadron and the Buffalos of No 67 were aided by an American Volunteer Group squadron flying Curtiss P-40s, and these were reinforced shortly after the Japanese invasion by another squadron of Blenheims and a number of Hurricanes to replace the outclassed Buffalos. These put up a strong resistance to the Japanese air attacks on Rangoon, and managed to cover the early stages of the army's withdrawal, but by April most of the surviving aircraft had been withdrawn for the defence of India itself.

In the event, apart from an attack on Ceylon in April 1942, the defenders of India had little to do. No air raids were mounted against Calcutta until December, and the arrival of a flight of radar-equipped Beaufighters in January 1943 soon halted these: six out of nine bombers on two separate raids were shot down, and no more were attempted. Consequently, there was time to re-organise the air forces, and to plan the ultimate defeat of the Japanese in Southeast Asia.

Hurricane and Thunderbolt, air support for the ground forces in Southeast Asia

The first requirement as far as the air forces were concerned was a massive increase in strength, and a corresponding provision of new airfields. A programme of airfield building begun at the end of March 1942 made slow progress at first, but by the end of the year five were operational, while another 850 or so single-runway and fair-weather landing strips were in use. By November 1943 the number of airfields with two runways had risen to 275, apart from further landing strips.

At the same time, the number of squadrons showed a steady increase, with new fighter, dive-bomber and reconnaissance units bringing the number up to 26 in March, compared with only five in the whole of India three months earlier. The dive-bomber squadrons were equipped with the Vultee Vengeance, the RAF's only purpose-built dive-bomber, which had been ordered from the American firm in 1940 after the German Stukas had proved so impressive in the early German blitzkriegs. By the time deliveries were under way the shortcomings of the dive-bomber – its vulnerability and the need for fighter escorts to allow it to operate without interference – had been realised, and the type was used operationally only in the Far East.

In support of the subsequent Allied offensives in Burma, however, the Vengeance gave extremely useful service. One technique developed in Burma involved the use of bombs with delayed-action fuses, set for varying intervals so that bombs continued to explode at unpredictable times after the attack was over. When the ground troops were preparing an attack, the bombs would be dropped without any fuse at all, allowing the men on the ground to advance in safety while the defenders waited for the explosions to start. The Vengeance was armed with five 0.5-in machine guns, two in each wing and one in the rear of the two-man cockpit, and could carry up to 2000 lb (907 kg) of bombs.

One reason for the ability of the Vengeances and Hurricanes, which carried out most of the ground-support attacks, to operate with relative freedom was the withdrawal of the bulk of the Japanese air forces from Burma to help counter American pressure on other fronts after May 1943. In October of that year Allied air superiority over Burma was further strengthened by the arrival of the first Spitfire squadrons, whose first task was to stop the Japanese photographic reconnaissance flights, whose interception had proved beyond the ability of the Hurricanes. Photo-reconnaissance Spitfires had begun operations over the Burma front the previous November.

Meanwhile, reconnaissance over the Bay of Bengal was carried out by Catalinas and Hudsons based in Ceylon. The Consolidated Catalina was used in substantial numbers by the RAF, and the type really came into its own in the Pacific and Indian Ocean, where its range of over 3000 miles (4830 km) in the reconnaissance role came in particularly useful. Blenheims previously employed for coastal patrols were replaced by Beauforts during 1942, and by February 1943 the

first squadron of Liberators was supplementing their efforts. The arrival of the Liberator squadrons had been delayed when they were pressed into service in the Middle East to support the Alamein offensive, and it was not until September 1943 that the first Liberator bombing unit was able to begin operations. Two squadrons of Wellingtons had begun operations the previous year, though one of these was engaged on supply dropping and training with airborne forces for several months after its arrival. Another achievement during 1942 was the creation of a network of radar stations along the Burmese border, with control centres at Calcutta and other places, including the main forward base at Imphal. With the establishment of maintenance and supply depots, the air force was rapidly reaching a useful operational capability.

During the second half of 1942 Japanese defences and British preparedness were tested by the first Arakan offensive along the coastal strip of Burma. A planned element of this offensive had been the capture of the Japanese airfield on the island of Akyab – one of the locations where the retreating British air elements had regrouped briefly during the retreat from Burma the year before – but the necessary landing craft for the operation had been retained in the Middle East. By September the land advance had already begun. Ultimately, the offensive proved beyond the capacity of the available force, but pressure from above meant that the retreat was postponed until the end of March 1943, when the position finally became untenable.

At the same time as the Arakan offensive was becoming bogged down, another operation of novel and daring conception was mounted behind the Japanese lines to the north. This was the famous expedition of the Chindits – officially the Long-Range Penetration Brigade – led by Colonel Orde Wingate, and deriving their familiar name from operations on the Japanese side of the Chindwin river. Each of the eight columns which made up the 3000-strong force was accompanied by an RAF radio detachment: the basis of Wingate's plan was that they should be able to operate independently in Japanese-occupied territory, relying on supplies dropped by air. The Dakotas of No 31 Squadron and the Hudsons of No 194 were responsible for carrying out the supply drops and it was this element of the operation which was to prove most significant for the future campaign in Burma.

During the remainder of 1943 the build-up of strength continued, with the ageing Blenheims replaced by Hurricanes for close support work and several squadrons of Spitfires arriving. In November a new command was formed for Southeast Asia, and the air forces of Britain and the United States were combined in the Eastern Air Command, which was in turn divided into strategic, tactical and troop carrying arms.

By mid-1944 the headquarters element of Eastern Air Command comprised a fighter wing with two squadrons of Spitfires and one of Beaufighters, plus a photographic reconnaissance force including two RAF

Right: Bristol Blenheim IVL, with long-range fuel tanks in the wings

squadrons, one with Spitfires and the other with Mosquitos and Mitchells, plus three American squadrons using Lightnings, Warhawks and Liberators. The Strategic Air Force included four USAAF squadrons of Liberators and another of Mitchells, while the RAF contributed three squadrons of Liberators, one of Wellingtons and an air-sea rescue squadron with Vickers Warwicks, the latter type having been designed originally as a replacement for the Warwick but serving instead in the rescue role.

The 3rd Tactical Air Force combined a substantial American Transport and long-range bomber group, the latter including four squadrons of Mitchells. The seven squadrons of Dakotas included in 3rd TAF, however, were later absorbed into the Combat Cargo Task Force which replaced the Troop Carrying Command which had been dissolved in June with the start of the monsoon season. Also included in the CCTF were eight RAF transport squadrons equipped with Dakotas. The remainder of 3rd TAF comprised RAF and Indian Air Force elements, amounting to 11 squadrons of Hurricanes, five of Spitfires, two using Vengeance dive-bombers and one with Beaufighters, plus an American squadron with Lockheed Lightnings.

Eastern Air Command itself formed part of Southeast Asia Command. Apart from the two special-duty squadrons using Hudsons, Liberators and Catalinas to infiltrate and supply agents and special forces operating behind enemy lines in occupied Malaya and Sumatra, the remainder of the overall command comprised the reconnaissance force of maritime patrol

types based on Ceylon, plus the nine squadrons responsible for defending the rest of India.

By this stage, Eastern Air Command already had some impressive achievements to its credit. In November 1943, simultaneously with the formation of the new organisation, a second offensive had begun in Arakan. This time concerted bombing of Japanese airfields, supply centres and other strategic targets by the Wellingtons and Liberators formed the background to the advance into Burma, and the Japanese forces were thwarted in their attempts to cut off and destroy the 7th Indian Division as a result of regular supplies being flown in to the beleaguered force. Vengeances were able to provide protection from Japanese air attack and dive-bombing, allowing a relief force to re-open the lines of communication so that the Japanese were defeated in Arakan by the end of February 1944.

By this time, however, the Japanese had launched their own offensive, and by 9 March Imphal was under attack. The latter was reinforced at great speed with the aid of Dakotas diverted from other duties, but then supplying the strengthened garrison became a problem. The heavy American C-46 Commandos, normally used for supplying the armies in China, were too much for the runways at Imphal, which were in any case frequently rendered unusable by the weather: only by piling up stocks at alternative points then ferrying them in when the weather relented could even minimal rations for the defenders be maintained.

Finally, the road to Imphal was opened again on 22 June. By this time the transports had flown in

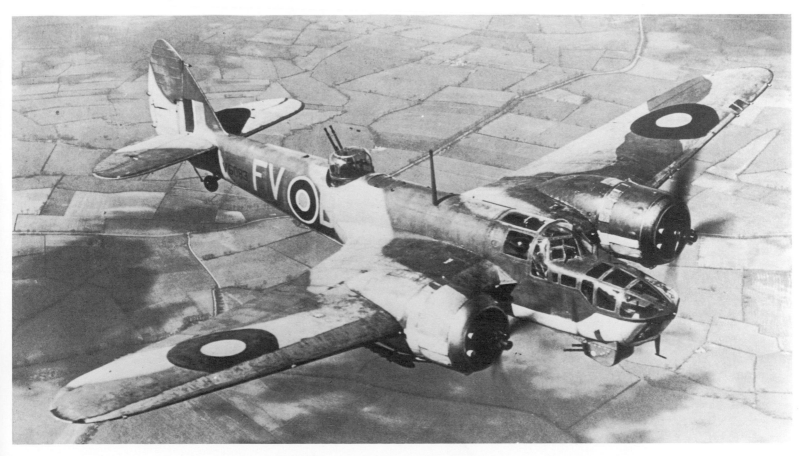

12,561 men and nearly 19,000 tons (19,304,000 kg) of supplies, and 13,000 casualties and 43,000 non-combatants had been airlifted out. Both aircrew and ground handlers were near collapse by this stage, and Imphal could not have held out much longer. Without the airlift it could not have survived at all.

The same was true at Kohima, where the defenders were besieged in a much smaller area following the start of the Japanese attack on 4 April. Kohima's position on an exposed ridge surrounded by mountains made the dropping of supplies extremely difficult. Nevertheless, while Hurricane and Vengeance attacks helped keep the attackers at bay, the Dakotas flew in regularly, dropping their cargoes from as low as 200 ft (61 m) above the ridge in order to minimise the risk of missing a position no more than a few thousand square yards in area. Fortunately for the defenders, the siege lasted only 13 days before relief arrived.

While the battles of Imphal and Kohima were raging, the Chindits were mounting a new and much more ambitious expedition. This time a force of 10,000 was to be flown deep into occupied territory by glider, while a further 2000 infiltrated the area on foot. The initial airborne element was to be transported in 80 gliders towed two at a time by Dakotas: these were to prepare landing grounds for the remainder to be flown in.

There were considerable casualties during the first phase, when a number of tow ropes broke and several gliders crashed: in fact, only 35 of the 61 gliders that took off on the first night reached their target. However, most of the Chindits were flown in by Dakota, and the various columns were kept supplied by air, while their casualties were flown out in light liaison aircraft and the RAF officers attached to each column were able to call in and direct bombing support. The exact value of the operation is difficult to assess: by the beginning of July the Japanese were in retreat after the defeats at Imphal and Kohima, and it has been claimed that the effort needed to support the Chindits could have been better used in those battles. On the other hand, the disruption caused by the Long-Range Penetration forces was certainly regarded as serious by the Japanese themselves, and in view of the narrowness of the margin of victory in the main battles, may have been decisive.

In any case, the air support was crucial to the success of the Allied cause, not only in the Arakan and on the central front, but also in support of the Chinese forces, under General Joseph Stillwell, which were

fighting their way down from North Burma. During the remainder of the campaign in Burma, which resumed in November after the rains had passed, RAF units achieved a high degree of specialisation in their support of the ground advance.

The strategic offensive continued, with attacks by the Liberators, which had finally replaced the last of the Wellingtons, being concentrated on the Burma-Siam railway which formed the principal Japanese supply route. Eventually raids were commonly carried out on targets more than 2000 miles (3220 km) from the Liberators' bases, and the introduction of the Azon guided bomb enabled many bridges to be destroyed. This comprised a standard 1000-lb (454-kg) bomb fitted with a radio receiver, steerable fins and a flare for tracking, so that an operator aboard the launch aircraft could guide it to its target.

The coastal patrol squadrons, meanwhile, were beginning to concentrate their efforts on the destruction of shipping off the Burmese coast, supplementing direct attacks with the laying of mines as far afield as Singapore. The photographic reconnaissance units, meanwhile, enabled detailed maps of the whole theatre to be compiled.

The most important aspect of the air contribution, however, was in direct support of the advancing ground troops. Republic Thunderbolts had begun to supplement the older fighter-bombers, providing a dramatic increase in close-support firepower. The Thunderbolt could carry a maximum of 2500 lb (1134

kg) of bombs, with a typical load consisting of a single 1000-lb (454-kg) bomb under each wing and another of 500 lb (227 kg) under the fuselage, and was armed with eight 0.5-in machine guns. The standard tactic for the Thunderbolt was the cab-rank patrol developed by the original tactical air force in the Western Desert. In a neat reversal of the original battlefield use of aircraft, when they flew above the front lines signalling map references to the artillery batteries below, the cab-rank patrols would loiter in the vicinity of the ground battle, waiting to be called into action by a controller on the ground.

By this stage of the campaign, the degree of air superiority provided by the Allied fighters was so nearly absolute that even Liberators were used in close support operations, delivering their heavier weight of bombs against enemy strongpoints. At the same time, Hurricanes continued to be used for close support, supplemented by the Spitfires which now had little opposition in the air.

Most important of all, however, was the supply operation without which the entire campaign could not have been fought. The steadily increasing distance from the main supply bases in Northeastern India led to the construction of new airfields as the advance progressed, each airfield being able to forward supplies over a radius of 250 miles (403 km). In the final stages of the advance on Rangoon, in April 1945, airfields were constructed every 50 miles (80 km), to serve as the base for the next leg.

The Consolidated Catalina was used extensively in the Indian Ocean for coastal patrol and other duties

11 TRAINING AND TRANSPORT

The Royal Air Force reached a peak strength in personnel of 1,185,833 in July 1944, 10 times the corresponding number of only five years before. The number of aircraft on charge in 1945 was, at its peak, 55,469: of these 9200 were first-line machines, more than three times the total number on strength in 1939.

One of the principal problems involved in the massive expansion described by these figures was the training of aircrew. Some progress had been made since the beginning of rearmament in the mid-1930s by the formation of the RAF Volunteer Reserve, members of which were trained at civilian flying schools under contract with the Air Ministry. However, with a wartime production rate of aircraft planned to reach 2500 a month the Volunteer Reserve could hardly be regarded as more than a starting point.

The answer was provided in the form of the Empire – later Commonwealth – Air Training Scheme, under which many thousands of aircrew were trained. The scheme began operation in May 1940 with the first schools for the training of RAF pilots in Canada, and eventually there were a total of 92 such schools when the scheme reached its peak in 1943. The scheme was expanded to include further establishments in Australia, New Zealand, South Africa, Southern Rhodesia and India, as well as Egypt, India, the United States and the Bahamas.

To deal with the demand not only for aircrew but also for skilled men in no fewer than 350 different trades, Training Command was divided to form separate branches to deal with flying and technical training. The latter was responsible for schools teaching everything from chaplaincy to bomb disposal as well as supplying the trained staff to deal with the aircraft and their associated equipment. Of course maintenance became at once more difficult, as aircraft in much greater numbers were subject to war damage as well as normal wear and tear; more complex, because the aircraft themselves were more complex,

and more urgent, because they were needed back with their squadrons as soon as possible.

To deal with these problems, Maintenance Command was formed in April 1938, and during the war its four groups were responsible for all the equipment used. No 40 Group, operating its own railways and goods yards to deal with a turnover of stores that reached well over 300,000 tons (3,048,000 kg) a month in 1944, provided the Aircraft Equipment Depots. These dealt in all forms of equipment except bombs, explosives, aviation fuel and oil, which were the responsibility of No 42 Group, whose turnover rose from 1,000,000 tons (1,016,000,000 kg) in 1943 to over 3,000,000 tons (3,048,000,000 kg) the following year. No 41 Group received the aircraft from factories, and after inspection and the installation of any additional equipment the new aircraft were delivered to squadron bases by pilots of the Air Transport Auxiliary.

Finally, No 43 Group was responsible for the repair of the aircraft and any other equipment. These were retrieved, either from their bases or from locations where they had crashed, by salvage units, and apart from the turnover in aircraft the Repair Depots turned out large numbers of repaired and reconditioned engines.

A substantial number of aircraft were damaged as a result of accidents during pilot training, and in consequence the training schedule was revised during the war, especially for pilots destined to fly the complex four-engined bombers. The average flying time on training before the war was 146 hours, after which pilots would receive operational training with an active squadron. During the war the squadrons were too preoccupied with operations to continue this system, and following the normal basic training of 50 hours on Tiger Moths or Miles Magisters, and a further 110 hours on Miles Masters, North American Harvards or Airspeed Oxfords, trainee pilots would then spend another 40 hours on operational types at an

Above: De Havilland Tiger Moth, used for elementary flying training

Previous page: Air-to-air gunnery practice in an Airspeed Oxford, with a target drogue towed by a Fairey Battle

Operational Training Unit. The Harvard was the standard advanced trainer with the Commonwealth Air Training Plan, the Master was the other standard single-engined advanced trainer, and the twin-engined Oxford was flown by pilots intended for multi-engined operational types, superseding the Anson for this purpose.

Later in the war this syllabus was expanded using the facilities of the overseas training schools. By 1944 a Lancaster pilot could expect to spend the best part of two years in training. After two months at an aircrew reception centre or initial training wing, during which 12 hours would be spent on Tiger Moths for assessment of aptitude, the trainee would spend 30 weeks overseas, during which he would spend at least 60 hours on basic trainers, followed by 155 hours on an advanced trainer. Further training on return to Britain might comprise another 80 hours on advanced trainers, followed by 80 hours on an operational type,

40 hours on a multi-engined type at a Heavy Conversion Unit, and a final 12 hours on a Lancaster at finishing school.

In the early stages of the war heavy bombers normally carried two pilots, but the demand was such that in March 1942 this was reduced to one. At the same time, his job was made easier by the addition of an automatic pilot, and a flight engineer was introduced who was also trained to land the aircraft in an emergency. The tasks of the other crew members were also revised. The observer became the navigator, and since he would be occupied with the new navigational equipment, bomb-aiming was taken over by another member of the crew who would also act as front gunner. The previous requirement for all air gunners to be trained as radio operators was also dropped: only one air gunner in each crew was also a radio operator, and others were gunners only.

A tenth home command was formed during the war.

Left: North American Harvards were among the most widely used trainers of the war years

Below: The RAF's first monoplane trainer, the Miles Magister entered service in 1937. This example is preserved by the Shuttleworth Trust

Ferry Command came into being in July 1941, succeeding the Atlantic Ferry Organisation. The latter was inaugurated in 1940 in order to speed up the delivery of new aircraft from the United States. The first aircraft used in what was a highly ambitious scheme for that time were Lockheed Hudsons, whose journey from the Lockheed factory in California had been taking up to three months by ship. Under the aegis of the Canadian Pacific Railway, the initial organisation was set up in Montreal in July 1940, and in November the first seven Hudsons made the crossing from Newfoundland to Northern Ireland.

Before April 1941, because of American neutrality, deliveries from California to the Canadian border had been made by civilians, but following the passage of the Lease-Lend Act it became possible for USAAF pilots to fly the aircraft direct to Montreal. This became the headquarters of the AFO, and Gander in Newfoundland and Prestwick in Scotland became the principal departure and arrival airfields. Hudsons were joined by Catalinas, Fortresses and Liberators on the direct crossing, and with the creation of a new base in Labrador it became possible to fly intermediate-range types in stages via Reykjavik, in Iceland. With American participation in the war, a further staging post was established in Greenland to enable fighters to be flown, rather than shipped, across the Atlantic. Subsequently, a second route was established for the delivery of aircraft to the Middle East, involving a journey via the Caribbean, Brazil and Ascension Island in the South Atlantic to the West African coast, and then across North Africa to Egypt.

In March 1943 Ferry Command became No 45 Group of the new Transport Command, whose other components were No 44 Group, dealing with transport based in Britain, No 216 in the Middle East and No 179 Wing in India. Subsequently, No 279 Group was formed in the Southeast Asia Command, and No 114 under Air Headquarters, West Africa. Meanwhile, another development was the formation of No 46 Group for the transport of airborne forces, for which No 38 Group of Fighter Command was also created.

The airborne forces groups used not only transport and heavy bomber types for carrying paratroops, but also gliders for guns and vehicles. The principal gliders were the American WACO Haig, known as the Hadrian in the RAF, which could accommodate up to 13 troops or light vehicles such as jeeps; the General Aircraft Hamilcar, designed to carry light tanks; and the Airspeed Horsa, with room for 26 troops or a variety of other loads such as jeeps, 25-pdr guns or parts for combat bridges. Towing aircraft used included Albemarles, Halifaxes, Stirlings and Dakotas.

The Dakota was also one of the principal general transport aircraft used by Transport Command, the RAF having no aircraft of this type at the start of the war apart from the obsolete bomber-transports of the 1930s. The first purpose-built British heavy transport aircraft was the Avro York, a development of the

Lancaster bomber with a completely new fuselage. The first Yorks became available in 1943, the third prototype being fitted out as a flying conference room for the personal use of the prime minister. In its normal configuration, with 24 passengers, the York had a range of 2700 miles (4345 km).

The airborne forces groups served in the landings in Sicily, in Normandy, at Arnhem and during the Rhine crossing in 1945. In the preliminary stages of the D-Day landings, more than 4000 paratroops were dropped, while nearly 500 arrived by glider with 17 guns, 44 jeeps and 55 motorcycles, as a result of the activities of Nos 38 and 46 Groups. For the Arnhem landing a total of 616 gliders were despatched in two waves, with 14 squadrons supplying the tow aircraft, while paratroops were dropped by American Dakotas. For the Rhine crossing a total of 440 gliders were used.

Left: Hudsons destined for Coastal Command await dispatch from the Lockheed plant in California. Hudsons were the first type to be flown, rather than shipped, to Britain

Below: WACO Hadrian troop-carrying gliders in a flooded field near Eindhoven in Holland

Another aspect of wartime transport was the clandestine operations carried out to drop and pick up agents in occupied Europe, and to supply arms, ammunition and other equipment to the resistance forces in France and elsewhere. The original unit carrying out these tasks in support of the resistance movement in France was No 138 Squadron, joined in February 1942 by No 161. Whitleys were the first type used for dropping agents and stores, often carrying bombs which were released over communications targets to disguise the true nature of their missions. As the war progressed, Havocs, Hudsons, Stirlings and Halifaxes also came into use, while for retrieving agents from occupied France the Lysander came into its own, its short take-off and landing ability making it eminently suitable for flying in and out of improvised landing strips in confined spaces.

12 AIRLIFTS AND EMERGENCIES, 1945-56

With the surrender of Japan in August 1945 and the end of the Second World War, transport became one of the RAF's main tasks. By the beginning of 1946 an average of 9000 passengers a month, mainly repatriated prisoners of war and replacements for staff at overseas bases, were being carried to and from the Far East. As well as Dakotas and Yorks, large numbers of converted Stirlings and Halifaxes were employed for these duties. Initially, transport versions of the heavy bombers simply had the gun positions faired over and carried baggage in the bomb bays, but special transport versions of both Stirling and Halifax were produced.

In January 1946 Transport Command's 42 squadrons and five flights were operating well over 1000 aircraft. In Britain three squadrons each of Stirlings and Yorks and another of Dakotas were operating internal routes, while one each of Dakotas and Warwicks covered European theatre communications. Four squadrons of Dakotas served in the Middle East, and 11 squadrons of Dakotas, supplemented by one each of Liberators and Douglas Skymasters, the military counterpart of the DC-4 civil airliner as the Dakota was of the DC-3, were based in India and Southeast Asia. In addition, six squadrons of Liberators, three of Dakotas and one of Yorks were engaged in trooping flights between India and the UK, while another squadron of Dakotas operated the Australia-Japan service. Six squadrons of Halifaxes were still assigned to airborne forces, three in the UK, two in the Middle East and one in Southeast Asia.

In common with other commands, however, Transport Command was to lose many of these units during the next year. However repatriation was not the only duty it was called on to perform. Sunderland squadrons based at Singapore were busy distributing food and medical supplies throughout the Far East during 1946, and within the next few years there was to be a great deal of movement as the British forces were withdrawn from the former outposts of the empire.

In 1947 India was partitioned to form the independent states of India and Pakistan, and the bulk of British forces were withdrawn, leaving behind only a limited number of advisers helping with the formation of new armed forces. The same year saw British control of Palestine, never particularly firm, become impossible, and from May 1948 the country was partitioned, again with an accompanying British withdrawal. Burma, too, became independent in 1949, and in February of that year there was an evacuation of women and children by a Sunderland of No 209 Squadron.

Nearer home, there was the problem of administering the defeated Axis states. In Italy, which had surrendered in 1943, but where fighting against the Germans had continued until May 1945, the principal problem was disposing of the stocks of explosives left behind by the various forces. Germany, however, presented a more complicated problem, being divided into four zones occupied by Soviet, American, British and French forces. The capital, Berlin, although inside the Soviet zone, was similarly divided.

The British Air Forces of Occupation consisted of No 2 Group, formerly of Bomber Command and the 2nd Tactical Air Force, along with some other elements of 2nd TAF, and their immediate task was disarming the Luftwaffe. This process, known as Operation Eclipse, involved processing nearly a million people, disposing of 5000 aircraft and destroying 220,000 tons (223,520,000 kg) of munitions and 195,000,000 rounds of ammunition. In March 1948, however, the Soviet administration began to restrict access by road to the non-Soviet zones of Berlin, and when road traffic was stopped completely in June, RAF and USAAF aircraft were pressed into service to supply the city by air.

The RAF contribution consisted of an eventual total of 40 Yorks, 40 Dakotas and 14 Handley Page Hastings transports. The last was a purpose-built military transport first flown in 1946; the first examples entered service in 1948, and along with later models served until 1968. Sunderland flying boats were also used in the early stages of the airlift, flying between the River Elbe and the Havel lake in Berlin, until the waters froze over. At the same time, a Combined Airlift Task Force was formed to co-ordinate British and American flights, and by the time the blockade was officially lifted in May 1949 the RAF had carried nearly 300,000 tons (304,800 tonnes) of supplies and nearly 70,000 passengers in just under 50,000 flights.

Above: The Avro York, a passenger development of the Lancaster bomber, which was used extensively during the Berlin airlift

Previous page: Hawker Hunter FGA.6 ground-attack fighter with No 229 Operational Conversion Unit in 1974

As well as these demonstrations of its new capacity for large-scale transport operations over long distances, the RAF in the immediate post-war years was also returning to some familiar pre-war scenes in its old peace-keeping and anti-terrorist role. In Indonesia, liberated from Dutch rule by the Japanese and then from the Japanese invaders, three squadrons of Mosquitos and two of Thunderbolts from Singapore were involved in action against insurrections fomented by the Dutch.

In the following year a new series of operations, code-named Firedog, was started in support of army counter-terrorist operations in Malaya. Ironically, the terrorists were members of the resistance organisation trained and equipped by the British during the Japanese occupation who refused to surrender their arms in 1948 and started a guerrilla campaign using arms supplied by China. The ensuing state of emergency was not finally lifted until 1960, and in the intervening 10 years the campaign was to see some interesting innovations.

Initially, the RAF's contribution consisted mainly of ground attacks by Mosquitos, Beaufighters, Ansons and Sunderlands, supported by Dakota transports. Photo-reconnaissance Spitfires and Mosquitos also photographed large areas of the peninsula until replaced by Meteor FR.10s, the PR version of the Meteor F.8 fighter-bomber, in November 1953.

Another jet fighter-bomber to serve in Malaya was the de Havilland Vampire in its FB.5 and FB.9 versions. The Vampire was the RAF's second jet fighter: it entered service with Fighter Command in March 1946, and was armed, like the Meteor, with four 20-mm cannon. By 1950 Vampires were in service with five regular and one Auxiliary Air Force squadron in the UK, as well as equipping all four fighter squadrons in Germany, where the BAFO had reverted to its earlier title of 2nd Tactical Air Force. In the Middle East another five squadrons were equipped with Vampires.

Although jet powered, the Vampire was not a sophisticated aircraft by contemporary standards, having no radar or power-operated controls, and its main use was as a two-seat trainer. The first two-seat version was a private venture night fighter with radar. This model was ordered by Egypt, but taken over by the RAF after an embargo on arms exports to Egypt, and served as the NF.10 until replaced by De Havilland Venoms and night fighter versions of the Meteor. The Venom was based on the Vampire, using the same twin-boom tail layout but with a 4850-lb (2200-kg) static thrust De Havilland Ghost engine in place of the much less powerful Goblin. This resulted in maximum speed being raised from around 550 mph (885 km/h) for the Vampire to 640 mph (1030 km/h).

Among the new piston-engined aircraft to serve in Malaya was one type specifically designed for the

The De Havilland Vampire F.1, the second jet fighter to enter RAF service

Far left: The Handley Page Hastings served with Transport Command for 20 years until 1968. This is one of a small number retained for signals work, photographed in July 1976

Left: Prototype of the Vickers Valetta transport, which entered service in 1948

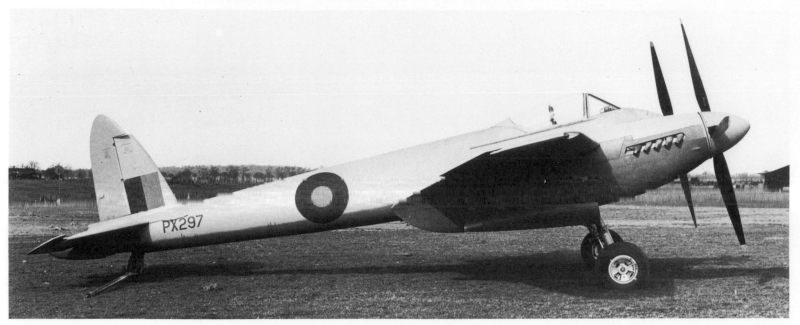

De Havilland Hornet F.3.
Originally designed for service in
the Far East, the Hornet was the
RAF's fastest piston-engined fighter

Far East. The De Havilland Hornet, derived from the Mosquito, was powered by two 2030-hp Merlins and with a maximum speed of 472 mph (760 km/h) was the fastest piston-engined aircraft to serve with the RAF. Using drop tanks the Hornet had a range of 2500 miles (4023 km), but its arrival was overshadowed by that of the new, and even faster, jet fighters, and only four home-based Fighter Command squadrons used it. Following its withdrawal from service in 1950, however, the F.3 fighter-bomber models, which could carry two 1000-lb (454-kg) bombs in addition to the standard armament of four 20-mm cannon, were shipped to the Far East, where they equipped three squadrons.

Serving alongside the Hornet in the ground-attack role in the early 1950s was the Bristol Brigand. The Brigand was originally built as a torpedo bomber replacement for the Bristol Beaufighter, and was designed to carry two torpedoes and a three-man crew. The first few produced were delivered to Coastal Command in this form, but it was then decided to adapt the type as a light bomber. With four 20-mm cannon and able to carry 2000-lb (907-kg) of bombs or rockets under the wings, it entered service in the Middle East in 1949, three years after its abortive start with Coastal Command.

The replacement for the Lancaster heavy bomber was another Avro design, the Lincoln. The Lincoln's original designation was Lancaster Mk IV, but it was a bigger, more powerful aircraft than its predecessor, able to fly at a much higher altitude and armed with twin 0.5-in Brownings in nose, tail and dorsal turrets. A large production programme was planned, but the first production examples did not appear until April 1945, and orders were reduced in consequence. There was little call for strategic bombing in the Malayan campaign, but a remarkable achievement of the type was the dropping of 200,000,000 leaflets over 200 separate terrorist positions in a single day in October 1953. This operation was carried out by one RAF and one RAAF squadron, both using Lincolns: the leaflets offered the guerrillas rewards if they surrendered.

Another method of broadcasting propaganda was the use of aircraft equipped with powerful loud-speakers to address the guerrillas directly. The first experiments were made with army co-operation Austers in November 1952, and the following year 2000-watt speakers were installed in Dakotas. These could be heard up to 2500 yards (2286 m) away from a Dakota flying at 2500 ft (762 m), so that by flying at just above stalling speed in a box pattern the messages could be rendered audible for continuous periods of 30 seconds.

In the early 1950s the Dakotas were replaced by the Vickers Valetta, a twin-engined transport based on the Viking commercial airliner. The Valetta could carry 36 people over a range of 290 miles (467 km), or two and a half tons (2540 kg) of freight 1600 miles (2575 km), and its main task was supply-dropping to ground forces.

For casualty evacuation in the Malayan jungle, helicopters were introduced in 1950 in the form of the Westland Dragonfly, a licence-built version of the

Right: The Westland Whirlwind,
based on the Sikorsky S-55, was
introduced by No 155 Squadron in
September 1954

American Sikorsky S-51. The Dragonfly could carry a pair of stretchers in special panniers, one on each side of the fuselage. This was rather a meagre payload, and considerably greater capacity was provided by the Westland Whirlwind, based on the Sikorsky S-55, which was first operated in Malaya by a Royal Navy squadron, before No 155 Squadron was formed with the type in September 1954. The Whirlwinds were used not only for cas-evac work, but also as troop carriers, and could carry up to 10 passengers or six stretcher cases.

One of the few British-designed helicopters to serve with the RAF, the Bristol Sycamore, also appeared in Malaya in 1954. Earlier deliveries had been made to Coastal Command for rescue work, and the Sycamore had half the carrying capacity of the Whirlwind. In this respect it had few advantages over the

Scottish Aviation Pioneer, which could fly with an airspeed as low as 36 mph (58 km/h) and could carry five passengers, or four soldiers with their equipment, or a stretcher case and attendant. Its short take-off and landing performance was also useful, and throughout 1955 the first six to arrive flew an average of well over two sorties a day.

Malaya was not the only area where the RAF was called on to suppress rebellion. In Kenya the activities of the mysterious Mau Mau organisation resulted in the proclamation of a state of emergency in 1952, and this remained in force until 1959. In the early stages of the anti-Mau Mau operations, Harvards were used to bomb suspected hideouts after being detached from training schools in Rhodesia and fitted with racks for 19-lb (8.6-kg) bombs. At the other end of the scale Lincolns were used to demonstrate the effects of 500-lb

Left: Loading a jeep through the cargo doors of a Valetta

Below: Iraqi air force De Havilland Venom FB.50, export version of the RAF's FB.1

A Hunting Percival Provost trainer
and its Jet Provost successor

Right: A Bristol Brigand equipped
for crew training with nose radome
and blacked-out rear cockpit

Far right: Gloster Meteor T.7
trainers

(227-kg) and 1000-lb (454-kg) bombs, though with little chance of hitting anyone that could hear them coming.

By the time of the Kenyan operations, the RAF was also involved in the Korean war, where the remarkable strides made by military aviation in the few years since the end of the Second World War were clearly demonstrated. While Sunderlands carried out coastal patrols and air-sea rescue missions, the first jet fighter combat was developing in the skies over Korea, as American F-86 Sabres fought North Korean MiG-15s. One result of the conflict in Korea, and the associated intensification of the Cold War, was an abrupt reversal of the rundown in RAF strength, with the number of aircraft in service being raised from 4510

English Electric Canberra T.17, electronic countermeasures training variant of the RAF's first jet bomber

Inset: A Canberra B.2 of No 57 Squadron in the mid-1950s

in 1950 to the post-war peak of 6338 in 1952, while the number of personnel in the service rose less dramatically to 277,000.

In the matter of equipment, a doubling of the rate of aircraft production was planned, with particular emphasis on the new English Electric Canberra. The twin-jet Canberra was the RAF's first jet-propelled bomber, and a major setback was the failure of the radar bombing system which had been specified. However, the Canberra's basic performance was such that the contemporary fighters were too slow to intercept it, and its introduction into service in 1951 was the start of a career that was to last well into the 1980s.

The original Canberra carried a typical bomb load of six 1000-lb (454-kg) bombs in an internal bay, but subsequent armament options included a gun pack mounting four 20-mm cannon under the fuselage and additional wing pylons for bombs or rocket pods. It was also built in photographic reconnaissance versions, and converted to produce electronic warfare, training and target models, as well as forming the basis for the Martin B-57 Night Intruder built in the United States for the USAF. By 1955 Canberras equipped 24 of the 31 Bomber Command squadrons based in Britain, and all four of the bomber squadrons with the 2nd TAF in Germany.

While the Canberra was under development, eight Lincoln squadrons were equipped with Boeing B-29 Superfortresses, which received the RAF name Washington. These were supplied under the Mutual

Defence Assistance Programme following the creation of the North Atlantic Treaty Organisation in 1949. Other aircraft supplied by the United States under the MDAP included four squadrons of Lockheed Neptune maritime patrol aircraft for Coastal Command in 1952. By this time flying boats, with their limited range and payload, had become outmoded: their great virtue of being able to operate without prepared airstrips had been nullified by the huge numbers of airfields constructed during the war.

Perhaps the most significant of the American imports in the early 1950s was the North American F-86 Sabre, built in Canada for the RAF. Experience in Korea with Meteors flown by Royal Australian Air Force squadrons showed that the British fighter was markedly inferior to the MiG-15, and with no successor to the Meteor in immediate prospect, Sabres were used to equip 10 fighter squadrons with the 2nd TAF in Germany and two Fighter Command units from 1952.

The first new British fighter to succeed the Meteor, Vampire and Venom was the Supermarine Swift. Despite setting a new world speed record of just under 738 mph (1188 km/h) in September 1953 the Swift was not a success. It equipped only one fighter squadron, though another two squadrons in Germany used photo-reconnaissance versions. In any case, the Swift had been ordered in the first place as insurance against

the failure of another new type, which in the event turned out to be one of the most successful of all jet fighter designs.

The Hawker Hunter entered service with Fighter Command in July 1954, and by 1958 all RAF day fighter squadrons in Europe were flying the F.6 version. Widely regarded as the best subsonic jet fighter ever built, the Hunter combined a top speed of 715 mph (1151 km/h) at sea level with the ability to climb to 45,000 ft (13,716 m) in just over seven minutes and a range in excess of 1800 miles (2897 km). Armament was four 30-mm Aden cannon, an overdue improvement on the early post-war standard of four 20-mm Hispanos, and for ground attacks the F.6 could carry two 1000-lb (454-kg) bombs or alternative weapons under the wings. The Hunter was also beautiful, and its exceptional manoeuvrability enabled the all-black examples used by No 111 Squadron as the Black Arrow to become the world's best aerobatic display team in the late 1950s.

Following the Hunter into service in 1956, the Gloster Javelin was the first purpose-built night fighter and all-weather interceptor provided for the RAF, and by 1960 it equipped 10 home-based fighter squadrons and another three in Germany. The original AI.10 radar was later replaced by the American APQ-43, and in 1958 the FAW.7 introduced Firestreak infra-red homing air-to-air missiles, the

Right: Trials of flight refuelling equipment for Valiant tankers: a Gloster Javelin takes fuel from a Canberra B.2

Below: Hawker Hunter F.6 of No 234 Operational Conversion Unit in April 1974

original gun armament of four Adens being reduced to two on this model. Performance was no more than moderate, with a maximum speed of 680 mph (1094 km/h), but the Javelin was well equipped and popular with its pilots.

In the same year as the Javelin entered service the RAF received its first jet transport aircraft in the shape of the De Havilland Comet C.2, a military development of the Comet I civil airliner offering the useful combination of accommodation for 44 passengers and a range of 2500 miles (4023 km). An electronics version was also built as the E.2.

Meanwhile, the development of a British nuclear bomb, the first test of which was carried out off northwestern Australia in October 1952, had been accom-panied by the issue of specifications for new bombers designed to carry the weapon. While the more advanced Victor and Vulcan were being developed by Handley Page and Avro, the Vickers Valiant was ordered as an interim carrier for the weapon, and the first production Valiant was delivered to the RAF in January 1955, entering squadron service later that year. The first operational atomic bomb was dropped by a Valiant on 11 October 1956; later the same month other Valiants were dropping conventional bombs in the opening round of Operation Musketeer, the ill-conceived Anglo-French-Israeli invasion of Egypt.

The nationalisation of the Suez Canal Company was the culmination of 10 years of growing Arab nationalism, that had involved the RAF in operations

in Aden and seen its withdrawal from some of its oldest bases in the Canal Zone. Apart from the French and Israeli units, amounting to 10 squadrons, and the carrier-borne units, an impressive RAF force was assembled for Musketeer. On Malta there were six squadrons of Canberras, four of Valiants and one of Shackletons, the maritime reconnaissance development of the Lincoln used by Coastal Command. On Cyprus there were another nine squadrons of Canberras, three each of Hastings and Valetta transports, four of Venom fighter-bombers, two of Hunters and one of Meteor night fighters, as well as another of photo-reconnaissance Valiants.

The campaign did not last long. On the night of 30 October and again the following morning Valiants bombed the Egyptian airfields, their attacks being followed up on the following four days by RAF and Fleet Air Arm fighter-bombers. On 5 November troops were landed by transport aircraft and by helicopter from the aircraft carriers and by midnight on 6 November international pressure had resulted in a cease-fire. On 22 December the last British and French troops left the occupied zone.

The Gloster Javelin all-weather fighter in its original configuration with four cannon in the wings

13 THE NUCLEAR DETERRENT

In 1957 the Conservative government announced a remarkable change in defence policy. A Defence White Paper published in April of that year outlined a new strategy based on the deterrent effect of the new nuclear weapons. Since it was considered impossible for manned interceptors to provide absolute immunity from enemy bombers carrying nuclear weapons, and since the consequence of even a small number of such bombers penetrating the air defences were considered to be unacceptable, it was decided that a reduced number of fighters should be committed to defending the bomber bases, which on the deterrent theory would comprise the basic defence of the country. Ultimately, it was predicted that the deterrent itself would be provided by ballistic missiles: in the meantime it was the job of the RAF to maintain the V-bomber force and ensure its survival in the event of war. In the longer term, the defence of the airfields would also be taken over by surface-to-air missiles.

By this time the second and third of the new bombers were in service. The Handley Page Victor adopted a crescent-shaped wing to enable it to meet the requirement for high subsonic speeds at high altitude, along with the ability to carry a 10,000-lb (4536-kg) weapon over a maximum range of 3500 nautical miles (4025 miles/6480 km). The Avro Vulcan, on the other hand, adopted a delta wing form to enable conventional stressed-skin construction techniques to be used. Whereas the Vulcan had a similar capacity to that of the Valiant for conventional bombs, each being able to carry a maximum of 21,000 lb (9526 kg), the Victor could carry as many as 35 1000-lb (454-kg) bombs.

The principal weapon of the three V-bombers, however, was to be the Blue Steel stand-off bomb, development of which was started in 1954. Fuelled by high-test peroxide and kerosene, Blue Steel was designed to be launched at a height of 35,000–40,000 ft (10,668–12,192 m): after release it was guided by an inertial navigation system, climbing to a greater altitude for its cruise towards the target, with a range in excess of 200 miles (322 km). The bomber would be free to take evasive action after releasing the weapon.

By the end of 1960 Bomber Command had 18 squadrons in service in the UK, seven of which were equipped with the Valiant, four each with the Vulcan and Victor and the remaining three with Canberras. Blue Steel did not enter service until 1964, however, and by this stage the operational requirement was changing. Speed and altitude were no longer sufficient protection for bombers, which were being forced to fly lower and lower in order to evade surveillance radars and surface-to-air missiles. Consequently, Blue Steel was modified so that it could be launched at a height of less than 1000 ft (305 m).

At the same time, the bombers themselves had to be modified to fit them for the new method of low-level penetration. A low-level version of the Valiant was designed and built in prototype form in 1953, but no production was ordered. By 1964, as a result of flying at low levels for which it had not been designed, the original B.1 model was beginning to show the strain by developing cracks in the wing spars, and rather than embark on an expensive programme of rebuilding and strengthening the wings the type was withdrawn. It had already been replaced in the quick-reaction strategic force by the Vulcan and Victor, and two squadrons were serving as tankers by this stage, with another three squadrons serving in the low-level tactical bombing role with the RAF's NATO forces in Germany.

The Victor and Vulcan, meanwhile, were progressively modified to equip them for the changing

The unmistakable shape of an
Avro Vulcan B.2 strategic bomber

The Vickers Valiant B.1 was the
first of the RAF's long-range
V-bombers to enter service

169

conditions in which they had to operate. The Mk 1A conversions of the original Victor and Vulcan provided improved electronic countermeasures equipment during the early 1960s, while more powerful engines were used in the B.2 versions designed to carry Blue Steel. By the end of 1965 Bomber Command's 12 home-based squadrons comprised three squadrons of Vulcan B.1s and six of the B.2 model, along with one squadron of Victor B.1As and two of Victor B.2s. The remaining squadron had the B(K).1A version of the Victor, which retained its bombing capability while also being equipped to provide in-flight refuelling.

In the following year the first Victor squadron converted to K.1 tankers, with three in-flight refuelling stations, and another two, including one reformed squadron, were subsequently equipped with tanker conversions. Another conversion of the Victor was the strategic reconnaissance SR.2, with cameras and other sensors in the bomb bay, which equipped one squadron from 1965. In mid-1966 the Vulcan force, which for the previous 12 years had been maintained in a state of constant readiness to deliver nuclear weapons, was switched to the low-level penetration role.

Meanwhile, in December 1958 the first Fighter Command squadron had become operational with the new Bristol Bloodhound surface-to-air missile. By the end of 1960 there were 12 squadrons using Bloodhounds, which carried a proximity-fused high-explosive warhead and were guided by radar pulses reflected from the target. By the end of 1964 the number of Bloodhound squadrons had been reduced to three, and these were equipped with the Mk 2 version whose continuous-wave semi-active radar guidance was more resistant to countermeasures. The Mk 2 was also faster, travelling at Mach 2, and had a longer range of 100 miles (161 km), though it also demonstrated an ability to intercept targets travelling at high speeds at under 1000 ft (305 m).

Bloodhound was joined in service towards the end of 1958 by the Douglas Thor intermediate-range ballistic missile, and another 19 squadrons were formed to operate the missile during 1959. With a range of 1725 miles (2776 km), a top speed of 10,000 mph (16,090 km/h), and a 1.5-megaton thermonuclear warhead, Thor was an advanced missile for its time, being the first ballistic missile to use inertial guidance, but it was quickly superseded by submarine-based intercontinental ballistic missiles. Consequently, the British weapons were deactivated in August 1963 and returned to the United States, where the rockets were subsequently used as boosters for space vehicles.

Above: Launch of a Bloodhound Mk 2 surface-to-air missile

Right: Test launch of a Thor, the missile which served briefly with the RAF in the late 1950s and early 1960s

Meanwhile, manned interceptors had not ceased to exist, and in 1961 the first RAF squadron became operational with the English Electric Lightning. Powered by two Rolls-Royce Avon engines, the Lightning had a top speed in excess of Mach 2, and was equipped with Ferranti Airpass radar. Armament consisted of two 30-mm Aden cannon plus two Firestreak missiles, another two Adens or pods of unguided air-to-air rockets. Progressive development of the original Lightning F.1 resulted in the F.2, with more powerful engines and flight refuelling probe, the F.3 with improved AI.23 radar and Red Top missiles and the F.6 with bigger fuel tanks and hardpoints on the wings for ferry tanks. The De Havilland Red Top is an improved version of the Firestreak with a more sensitive infra-red seeker capable of searching through wider angles – Firestreak would only home on jet exhausts if launched from behind the target aircraft – a bigger warhead, higher speed and longer range. Its improved performance reflected the increasing capabilities of the bombers Firestreak was originally designed to intercept, particularly low-flying aircraft travelling at high speeds.

By the middle of 1960, with the first Lightning squadron operational, Fighter Command in Britain deployed 10 squadrons of all-weather Javelins and seven of Hunters. Single squadrons of Hunters were stationed in Aden and at Nairobi in Kenya, while a squadron each of Venoms and Meteor night fighters were based at Singapore. The 2nd Tactical Air Force in Germany had three squadrons of Javelins and six of Hunters. By June 1965 these 32 squadrons had been reduced to only 19, with Fighter Command reduced to six squadrons of Lightnings. Transport Command in the UK operated two squadrons of Hunters, and RAF Germany, as the 2nd TAF had become, had only two squadrons of Javelins. The Near East Air Force, as the former Middle East Air Force had been renamed in 1961, had one squadron of Javelins on Cyprus, while three squadrons of Hunters were serving with the Aden Strike Wing. The Far East Air Force had two squadrons of Javelins and one of Hunters at Singapore, with another squadron of Hunters in Hong Kong.

There were several other organisational changes during this period. In September 1957 the Army Air Corps was formed; in 1958 No 90 (Signals) Group became Signals Command, a title which it carried for the next 10 years before reverting to its old name. In 1960 No 38 Group was reformed within Transport Command as a self-contained tactical unit capable of

Above: De Havilland Firestreak
air-to-air missiles on a late-model
Javelin

Left: In-flight refuelling for a
Lightning F.1 from a Vickers
Valiant K.2 tanker

deployment by air to support the army in any part of
the world. While the long process of withdrawal from
overseas bases continued with the termination of the
RAF base in Ceylon, to be replaced by a new base on
Gan in the Maldive islands, there were a series of
deployments involving the RAF in operations throughout the world.

Transport Command was provided with a series of
new aircraft during this period. In 1956 the Blackburn
Beverley entered service as a medium-range freight
and troop carrier. With four engines and reversible-
pitch airscrews, the Beverley could land in as little as
225 yards (206 m). Its deep fuselage could accommodate up to 94 troops, 82 casualties or military loads
of up to 45,000 lb (20,412 kg) over a range of 230 miles
(370 km), or 1300 miles (2092 km) with a 29,000-lb
(13,154-kg) payload.

The Bristol Britannia, which was used under contract until 1959, when the first batch of a total of 22
were handed over to the service, was a four-engined
turboprop, the first such aircraft to be used as a long-
range transport. The Britannia could carry up to 115
troops with full equipment, while the Armstrong
Whitworth Argosy which joined it in service in 1961
could carry 69 troops, 54 paratroops or 48 stretcher
cases. In 1962 the first of five Comet C.4s was delivered:
bigger and with more powerful engines, the C.4
increased the original C.2's accommodation for 44
passengers to 94, and offered much longer range.

Longest range of all, however, was provided by the

BAC VC-10, which had an unrefuelled range of 3650
miles (5877 km) with 150 passengers or up to 76 stretcher cases. The year 1966, when the VC-10 entered
service, was also the year of the arrival of the Lockheed
Hercules. Able to carry 92 troops, 64 paratroops or 74
stretcher cases, the Hercules had a typical range of
2875 miles (4629 km), and a total of 66 were acquired
from the American manufacturers.

Other new transports to enter service in 1966 were
the Short Belfast and Hawker Siddeley Andover, both
military versions of civil passenger aircraft. At the
same time, the helicopter strength was increased for
tactical deployment of troops on the battlefield. The
Bristol Belvedere, originally designed for the Royal
Navy, entered RAF service in 1961. The turbine
installations for the Belvedere's twin rotors proved
inconvenient, however, and the 26 Belvederes built
lasted only a few years in service. More successful was
the later Westland Wessex, a licence-built version of
the American Sikorsky S-58, which entered service in
1964. Able to lift 16 troops, the Wessex HC.2 has also
been armed with anti-tank missiles and machine guns
for use against ground targets.

With all this new lifting capacity, the RAF was not
short of opportunities for its application. Some operations were occasioned by natural disasters, such as the
hurricane which devastated Belize, the capital of
British Honduras, in October 1960. The same year
saw Shackletons based at Gibraltar flying medical
supplies to Agadir, in Morocco, after more than 12,000

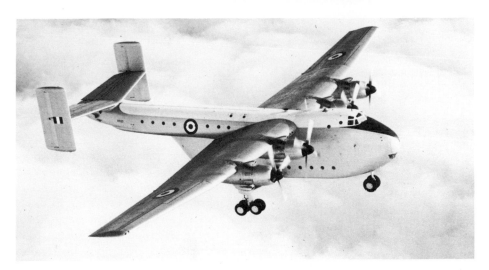

people had died in an earthquake, and in 1961 Beverleys were used to distribute food in northern Kenya and Somalia, which were suffering the effects of a drought in the early part of the year and floods the following autumn.

More often, though, the transports were called on to reinforce overseas garrisons in emergencies. In July 1960, just as the Malayan emergency was officially declared to be over, the United Nations force in the Congo was reinforced and supplied by Comets, Britannias and Beverleys, while two Hastings were stationed at Accra to support the Ghanaian Brigade. Transport Command aircraft also helped to evacuate refugees.

In 1961 appeals for help from the Emir of Kuwait, whose new-found independence was threatened by Iraqi forces, resulted in the deployment of British forces from Cyprus and Britain. Two squadrons of ground-attack Hunters flew in from Aden, and troops were airlifted from Bahrein. Canberras were transferred from Germany and Cyprus, and the whole force was supplied by a major airlift using all available types of transport aircraft based in England, Aden, Nairobi and the Far East. In the course of the operation, nearly 10,000 men and 850 tons (863,600 kg) of cargo were carried by air to Kuwait, though the distances involved emphasised the shortage of long-range transports, a situation remedied by the orders for the VC-10 and Belfast.

In May 1962 a squadron of Hunters was stationed in Thailand after incursions by Laotian troops, with supplies ferried in by Hastings and Beverleys. Towards the end of the year, the same squadron was transferred to the protectorate of Brunei in northern Borneo where a rebellion had broken out. Other units deployed in Brunei included Pioneers, which had been based on the island of Labuan while engaged on patrols to combat pirates, and Beverleys and Belvederes from Singapore, the transports flying in troops who were taken into action by the Pioneers and helicopters. However, the situation in Indonesia soon became worse, as Indonesian opposition to the proposed federation of Malaysia resulted in guerrilla attacks on Sabah and Sarawak.

As the violence in Indonesia became worse, Beverleys began to fly out British families from Djakarta in September 1963. The confrontation with Indonesia lasted until 1966, during which time British and Commonwealth forces were supplied by Wessex helicopters and by stores air-dropped from Beverleys and Argosy transports. In the course of the operations Canberras were used to deliver air strikes, and detachments of V-bombers were based at Singapore.

Other troop deployments carried out by the RAF during the early 1960s included British Guiana (now Guyana) in 1963; Kenya and Uganda in 1964; Mauritius in 1965; and, the two most serious, Cyprus and Aden. The outbreak of civil war in Cyprus, which had become independent in 1960 and which provided the bases for the Near East Air Force at Akrotiri and Dhekelia, resulted initially in the despatch of substantial reinforcements to the island. In March 1964 the United Nations took over responsibility for security on the island, and the multinational force was supported by RAF transport aircraft and helicopters.

In October 1959 the British Forces Aden Peninsula joint command was established, and replaced by Air Forces Middle East in February 1961. A bomb attack at Aden civil airport on an official party, including the High Commissioner and a number of ministers of the Federation of South Arabia, whose creation had been opposed by the neighbouring state of Yemen, signalled the start of a state of emergency. The complex political situation in the area did not offer any hope of immediate solution, and in the absence of a more constructive policy for the area it was decided to mount a large-scale military operation against insurgents in the Radfan area some 60 miles inland from Aden itself, close to the border with Yemen.

Three battalions of the Federal Regular Army were supported by Centurion tanks, Royal Engineers and a battery of artillery. The RAF contribution to the expedition comprised ground-attack Hunters from RAF Aden plus Shackletons to carry out bombing attacks and Belvedere helicopters to supply the troops.

The successful conclusion of the first campaign, whose object was to establish military control of the region, was followed by a withdrawal of the federal forces. These did not have the resources to sustain a military presence in the area as well as maintain the policing of the border with Yemen, and the disturbances immediately resumed.

Attacks across the border by Yemeni aircraft brought a retaliatory attack on a Yemeni border fort, and a new campaign was begun by a joint Federal-British force known as Radforce. Ultimately, as part of a general reduction of overseas commitments, and in the face of increasing terrorist activity, it was decided to withdraw from Aden altogether, and the final airlift began in May 1967. Initially, families of servicemen were flown out, and after the reduction of the Army and RAF strength to the minimum necessary to defend the base at Khormaksar, the final stage was completed in three days in November, when the remaining personnel were flown out by Hercules.

Because of the reduction of overseas bases, the role of the transport aircraft was becoming increasingly important, as it was intended to fulfill overseas commitments by the rapid deployment of forces as they were needed, rather than maintain permanent garrisons. As part of the resulting reorganisation, Transport Command was renamed Air Support Command in August 1967.

14 STRIKE AND SUPPORT

A further stage in the reorganisation of the Royal Air Force was reached in 1968, with the formation of Strike Command. Severe economies were also introduced, including the cancellation of the American F-111s ordered as replacements for the ageing Canberras after the British TSR.2 project had been abandoned. At the same time, the withdrawal from overseas bases was accelerated.

Fighter Command and Bomber Command were amalgamated to form the new organisation at the end of April. Strike Command's responsibilities were to include the various air defence functions, while Support Command was to be responsible for operations involving the ground forces. In November 1969 Coastal Command was also absorbed into Strike Command, while from June 1968 the flying training and technical training branches were combined in a single Training Command.

The maintenance of the V-bomber and in-flight refuelling squadrons became the responsibility of No 1 Group. By the end of 1970 the strike element consisted of two squadrons of Buccaneers, five of Vulcan B.2s and three of Victor tankers, all based in Britain. The Hawker Siddeley Buccaneer was originally produced for the Royal Navy, entering service with the Fleet Air Arm in 1962, and in its S.2 form, with Rolls-Royce Spey turbofans, it was ordered for the Royal Air Force in 1968 to replace the cancelled F-111s. In addition to the 43 new Buccaneers built for the RAF between 1970 and 1976, most of the Royal Navy's 84 S.2s were transferred from the Navy to the RAF following the retirement of most of the Navy's aircraft carriers.

By 1975 Buccaneers had also replaced the two squadrons of Canberras serving with RAF Germany. At the beginning of 1983 these were still in service, armed with Martel missiles. Martel exists in two versions, one using a television camera in the nose to enable the operator in the launch aircraft to guide it to its target, the other equipped with a radar-homing head. Buccaneers will be replaced in the strike role by the Tornado GR.1, and will then transfer to maritime strike duties, armed with the new Sea Eagle missile. The two UK-based Buccaneer squadrons will be converted to reconnaissance, using either infra-red sensors or cameras mounted on the bomb bay door.

During the early 1970s the V-bomber force was also revised. The two squadrons of Vulcan B.2s based in Cyprus in 1970 returned to Britain, and the Victor SR.2s were converted to tankers, a number of Vulcans in turn being converted for the strategic reconnaissance role. All the remaining Victor tankers had been retired by the end of 1982, and the remaining Vulcans, apart from the six converted as tankers for in-flight refuelling, were scheduled to follow them into retirement.

New fighters were also provided for Strike Command from 1968 in the form of McDonnell Douglas Phantoms. A total of 52 Phantom FG.1s were delivered, based on the US Navy's F-4J but with Rolls-Royce

Previous page: Third prototype of the Panavia Tornado, the RAF's principal tactical fighter for the 1980s

Left: A trio of McDonnell Douglas Phantom FG.1s of No 43 Squadron

Inset: A Buccaneer S.2 armed with a Martel TV-guided air-to-surface missile

Spey afterburning turbofans, of which 24 went to the Royal Navy for service aboard *Ark Royal*. Two RAF squadrons of Strike Command were equipped with the FG.1, while subsequent deliveries of 118 FGR.2s equipped three squadrons of Strike Command and four squadrons with RAF Germany by 1975. In 1982 a total of five home-based and two RAF Germany squadrons were using Phantoms.

The FG.1 was produced as an air defence interceptor, while the FGR.2 is a multi-role fighter, ground-attack and reconnaissance version. Both models can carry a wide range of armament, including an SUU-23 multi-barrel cannon and Sparrow or Sidewinder air-to-air missiles. For reconnaissance a sensor pod is carried below the fuselage in place of the gun, and for ground attack the Phantom can carry a variety of munitions including conventional high-explosive bombs, cluster bombs and rockets up to a total weight of 16,000 lb (7257 kg).

Following the Phantom into service in 1959, the British Aerospace Harrier introduced a completely new capability for a fixed-wing aircraft, namely the ability to take off and land vertically. In fact, the Harrier normally uses a short take-off run, since this enables a greater weight of fuel or stores to be carried. Nevertheless, it can operate from dispersed locations with the most basic facilities, making it particularly useful in the close-support role, where the main requirement is a quick reaction to requests for an air strike. Accordingly, the main RAF version of the Harrier was the GR.3 for service with RAF Germany, where the type equipped three squadrons by the mid-1970s. Armament options include two 30-mm Aden cannon carried in pods under the fuselage, or up to 5300 lb (2404 kg) of bombs, rockets or other weapons. The GR.3 has a laser range-finder in a nose fairing, and for service in the Falklands campaign, Sidewinder air-to-air missiles were fitted.

The two Harrier squadrons serving in Germany in 1982 were due to have their GR.3s replaced by the GR.5 model, the British designation for the AV-8B under development in the United States by McDonnell Douglas. The GR.5 will be able to carry double the payload of the GR.3, or a similar weapon load over greater distances. Equally important, it will provide improved attack aids and electronic countermeasures, thus increasing its ability to survive on a modern battlefield.

Below and right: British Aerospace Harrier GR.3s in their normal environment and on the deck of the aircraft carrier HMS *Hermes* in the South Atlantic in 1982

PRESENT-DAY RAF AIRFIELDS

Lossiemouth
Kinloss

Leuchars

Boulmer

Omagh

Leeming
Dishforth · Topcliffe
Linton-on-Ouse
Leconfield
Church Fenton · North Coates

Binbrook
Finningley

Valley

Scampton · Coningsby
Waddington · Cranwell
Shawbury Cottesmore West Raynham
Marham · Coltishall

Wittering
Wyton
Honington

Brawdy Benson Oakington Wattisham
Brize Norton
Lyneham

Chivenor Netheravon · Farnborough
Roborough Middle Wallop
Yeovilton Odiham
St Mawgan Wilton Lee-on-Solent

Portland

Culdrose

The principal RAF attack aircraft with RAF Germany during the 1970s was the Jaguar, developed jointly by British and French firms under the company name SEPECAT. The first Jaguars entered service in 1973, and despite the type's original conception as an advanced trainer with attack capability it has proved an extremely useful strike aircraft. Incorporating inertial navigation, an integrated navigation and attack system with head-up display and moving map projection, and a laser ranger and marked target seeker in the nose, the Jaguar had demonstrated its ability to find and attack targets with great precision, while offering outstanding reliability. Like the Buccaneers, the Jaguars in Germany are scheduled for replacement by the interdictor strike (IDS) version of the Tornado.

Supplementing the Lightnings and Phantoms of No 11 Group, which carried the responsibility for the air defence of Britain during the 1970s was the airborne early-warning version of the Shackleton. A total of 12 Shackletons, after 20 years service with Coastal Command and No 18 (Maritime) Group of Strike Command, were fitted with APS-20 search radar from 1971 to serve in the early-warning role while AEW.3 version of the Nimrod was being developed.

Aircraft in service

TYPE	NO.	ROLE *On order
Tornado F.2	165*	AD
Phantom FG.1/FRG.2	110	AD
Lightning F.3/F.6/T.5	50	AD
Buccaneer S.2	65	Strike
Tornado GR.1	70(220*)	Strike
Vulcan K.2	6	Tanker
Jaguar GR.1/T.2	92/24	Strike/recce
Harrier GR.3/T.4	71(23*)	Attack
Harrier GR.5	60*	Attack
Hawk T.1	128(46*)	Trainer
Hunter FGA.6/9	60	Trainer
Canberra	40	ECM/recce/trainer
Nimrod MR.1/2	32	ASW
Nimrod AEW.3	11*	AEW
Nimrod R.1	3	Elint
Shackleton AEW.2	8	AEW
Victor K.2	19	Tanker
VC10 K.3	9*	Tanker
Hercules C.1/C.3	26/30	Transport
Hercules CK.1	4*	Tanker
Andover E.3/CC.1/2	5/6	CAL/VIP
HS.125 CC.1/2	6	VIP
HS.125 Dominie T.1	19	Nav trainer
Devon CC.1	13	Liaison
Pembroke CC.1	6	Liaison
Jetstream T.1	11	Trainer
Jet Provost T.3/5	150	Trainer
Bulldog T.1	112	Trainer
Chipmunk T.10	50	AEF/trainer
Helicopters		
Chinook	27(3*)	Transport
Sea King	16	SAR
Puma	31(7*)	Transport
Wessex	46	Transport/SAR
Whirlwind	15	SAR/VIP/trainer
Gazelle	24/1	Trainer/VIP

Belly view of a SEPECAT Jaguar
tactical strike aircraft

Jaguar T.2 operational trainer

Jaguars and Phantoms in
formation

Prototype of the British Aerospace
Nimrod AEW.3

Right: One of No 33 Squadron's
Westland Pumas over Belize in
November 1975

Inset: Test launch of a Rapier
surface-to-air missile

The Nimrod itself was based on the Comet C.4, and
the first of the 38 built entered service in October 1969.
During the early 1970s four squadrons of No 18
Group, and a fifth squadron based on Malta, had their
Shackletons replaced by the initial MR.1 version of
the Nimrod. For maritime patrol and anti-submarine
work the Nimrod is equipped with radar, magnetic
anomaly detection gear and other sensors which are
operated by a 12-man crew. An unpressurised pannier
added on the underside of the fuselage provides accommodation for up to nine anti-submarine torpedoes as
well as depth charges, mines or bombs. Supplementary
fuel tanks can also be installed in the weapons bay,
and air-to-surface missiles can be carried on wing
pylons, though this is not usual.

The MR.2 Nimrod features improved radar and
data processing equipment, together with a new
acoustic signal processing unit for use in conjunction
with sonobuoys. Conversion of MR.1s to MR.2 standard began in 1975, and deliveries began in the late
1970s. Meanwhile, the airborne early-warning version, with nose and tail radar scanners, each scanning
through a 180° arc, was ordered in 1977. The programme was running several months late in the early
1980s, but the first deliveries were scheduled for 1983,
and the Nimrod AEW.3 is intended to replace both the
obsolete Shackletons and the strategic reconnaissance
version of the Vulcan. The Shackletons and Vulcans
are then intended to work in conjunction with the
Buccaneers when the latter begin operation in the
maritime-strike role, locating targets and directing the
Buccaneers to them.

The other main elements of No 18 Group are the
five flights of Wessex and four of Sea King rescue

helicopters based around the British coast. Another
Sikorsky design built by Westland under licence, the
Sea King entered service in the rescue role in August
1978. Other new helicopters to enter service during the
1970s were also of foreign origin. In 1971 the Puma,
designed by Aérospatiale in France and built for the
RAF by Westland, joined two squadrons as a tactical
transport. The Puma can accommodate up to 16 fully
equipped troops or six stretcher cases and is used both
in Britain and in Germany. The Boeing Vertol Chinook
offers considerably greater carrying capacity, with a
maximum payload of 21,700 lb (9843 kg), and during
the operations in the Falklands in 1982 the single
Chinook that escaped being sunk with the *Atlantic
Conveyor* carried 80 troops with additional mortars and
machine guns during the assault on Bluff Cove.

Prior to the Falklands conflict, RAF operations had
followed a familiar pattern, with frequent overseas
deployments to deal with emergencies or to help in
the relief operations in the aftermath of natural
disasters. One semi-permanent deployment was that
of a detachment of Harriers to Belize, to help guard
against an invasion by Guyanese forces. Another
continuing overseas commitment is the squadron of
Wessex helicopters stationed in Hong Kong to support
the local security forces.

Another Wessex squadron remains on Cyprus under
the United Nations force on the island. Cyprus was
also the scene of a major operation in 1974, following
the Turkish invasion. In the subsequent evacuation of
service families and the airlift of reinforcements for the
British garrison and supplies for the refugees more than
22,000 people had been flown out of the island aboard
RAF transports.

Meanwhile, the RAF's continuing role within NATO was to provide air defence of the British Isles, guard the Atlantic approaches and support the ground forces in Europe. In this context, it was hardly surprising that the requirements of the task force sent to the South Atlantic found the transport and tanker force heavily stretched. In the event, the gap was filled by the emergency conversion of Hercules transports to act as tankers. In the months following the task force's landing on the islands, the Hercules established a regular service to the South Atlantic via Ascension island.

In the longer term, the requirement for new tankers will be met by the conversion of six Lockheed TriStar wide-bodied airliners acquired from British Airways. As well as replacing the aircraft lost during the Falklands battles, the RAF will be provided with enough ex-US Navy Phantoms to form a new squadron, additional Chinooks and further Rapier surface-to-air missile units. The Rapier system entered service in 1964 as the RAF's low-level air defence system, and at the beginning of 1982 was operated by two squadrons of the RAF Regiment, which was formed in 1942 to provide the defence of airfields.

For the foreseeable future, however, the RAF's principal combat capability will be provided by the Panavia Tornado, developed by a joint British, German and Italian consortium and ordered for the RAF in both GR.1 interdictor strike and F.2 air defence variants. It is envisaged that 220 of the strike version will be provided to replace Vulcans and Buccaneers, and by the end of 1982 the first two squadrons were equipped with the Tornado GR.1. A further nine squadrons are scheduled to receive this model, while the F.2 is intended to replace the Lightnings and Phantoms in Britain, although two squadrons of Phantoms are to be retained. Further air defence capability will be provided by Hawk trainers armed with Sidewinders.

The Tornado represents an unprecedented degree of versatility in a modern combat aircraft. In the ground-attack role it can carry a wide range of weapons on three fuselage and four wing stations. Its integrated nav/attack system enables it to locate targets by day or night in all weathers, and on trials it has proved able to deliver bombs within 30 ft (9.1 m) of a 10-ft (3.05-m) target from as much as four miles (6.4 km) away in the toss-bombing mode. The flight control system incorporates fly-by-wire and a range of automated functions that permit strike missions to be flown at high speeds and very low levels. The air defence variant will be able to operate up to 400 miles (645 km) from its base in any weather conditions, using the new Foxhunter radar to identify even low-flying supersonic targets in spite of heavy ECM. A single 27-mm cannon will be carried (the IDS version has two) along with Skyflash and Sidewinder missiles. Future requirements may be unpredictable, but the Tornado has been designed to meet any that can be foreseen.

British Aerospace Hawk trainers spell out the name of their base with their tail codes

Left: A Boeing Chinook HC.1 demonstrates its ability to lift a nine-ton combat reconnaissance vehicle

INDEX

INDEX

ACKNOWLEDGMENTS

We would particularly like to thank the staff of the Imperial War Museum, the RAF Museum, Shorts, Vickers, Westland and the various sections of British Aerospace for their invaluable help with the pictures for this publication.

Picture research and prints were through Military Archive & Research Services, Braceborough, Lincolnshire and maps and diagrams by Pierre Tilley.

For reasons of space alone, some references have been abbreviated as follows:

British Aerospace-Aircraft Group: BAe
Crown Copyright (MOD-RAF): MOD
Imperial War Museum: IWM
Military Archive & Research Services: MARS
RAF Museum: RAF
Vickers Limited: Vickers

Front cover: MOD. P1: Blitz. 2–3: MOD. 4–5: Blitz. 6–7: IWM, 8–9: Air Portraits. 10–13: IWM. 14–15: M Jerram. 16–17: IWM. 18–19: James Gilbert. 20: BAe. 21: IWM. 22–23: BAe. 26–27: MARS. 28–29: BAe. 30: Vickers. 30–31: MARS. 32: Canadian Museum of Science & Technology. 33: IWM. 34–41: BAe. 42–45: RAF. 46: Vickers. 46–47 (top): Westland Ltd. 46–47 (btm): Vickers. 48–51: BAe. 52–53: RAF. 54–59: Shorts Ltd. 59: Vickers. 60–61: IWM. 62–71: BAe. 72–73: Vickers. 73: BAe. 74–75: Vickers. 76–77: RAF. 78–79: Vickers. 80–81: BAe. 82–83: RAF Club. 84–85: BAe. 86–87: R E Richardson. 88–89 (top): Vickers. 88–89 (btm): IWM. 89: BAe. 90: Vickers. 91: IWM. 92–93: MARS. 94–95: IWM. 96 (btm lt): BAe. 96–97: IWM. 98: M Jerram. 100: IWM. 101: BAe. 102: Popperfoto. 103 (top): BAe. 103 (btm): IWM. 104–105: Research House. 106–108: IWM. 110–111: Fox Photos. 112–113: IWM. 113–115: BAe. 116–129: IWM. 130–131: MARS. 132–135: IWM. 136–137: Shorts Ltd. 138–141: IWM. 143: BAe. 144–147: IWM. 148–149: BAe. 150–151: Lockheed Corp. 151: IWM. 152–153: MOD. 154–155 (top): BAe. 155 (btm lt): MOD. 155 (btm rt): Vickers. 156: BAe. 156–157: Westland. 157 (top): Vickers. 157 (btm): BAe. 158–159: BAe. 160–161: MOD. 162–163: MOD. 163: Flight Refueling. 164–169 (top): MOD. 169 (btm): Vickers. 170: BAe. 171: FMC. 172: BAe. 173–174: MOD. 175 (top & centre): BAe. 175 (btm): Lockheed Corp. 176–177: BAe. 177 (btm): Vickers. 178–189: MOD. 189 (btm): Boeing Vertol.